D0437371

What EVERY ARTIST and COLLECTOR should know about THE LAW

by Scott Hodes

with a Foreword
by
Professor Harold Haydon
The University of Chicago

A Dutton Visual Book

E.P. Dutton & Co., Inc. / New York / 1974

To my father who has been a constant source of inspiration.
S. H.

KF
390
.A7
H63

The author wishes to express his appreciation
to Nicolas Ducrot for his encouragement and support.

S. H.

Copyright © 1974 by Scott Hodes
All rights reserved. Printed in the U.S.A.
First Edition

10 9 8 7 6 5 4 3 2 1

No part of this publication may be reproduced or
transmitted in any form or by any means, electronic
or mechanical, including photocopy, recording, or any
information storage and retrieval system now known
or to be invented, without permission in writing
from the publisher, except by a reviewer who wishes
to quote brief passages in connection with a review
written for inclusion in a magazine, newspaper or
broadcast.

Published simultaneously in Canada by Clarke, Irwin & Company
Limited, Toronto and Vancouver
ISBN: 0-525-49501-0

Library of Congress Cataloging in Publication Data

Hodes, Scott.
  What every artist and collector should know about
the law.

  (A Dutton visual book)
  1. Law and art. I. Title.
KF390.A7H63   340'.02'47   74-6350

CONTENTS

57785

PART II: THE COLLECTOR

FOREWORD

Since the forerunner of this concise yet comprehensive guide through the legal maze appeared in 1966, much has happened in the art world to strengthen the view that no one—be he artist, artist's heir, collector, dealer, museum director, or museum trustee—can afford to be ignorant of the law as it applies to the production, marketing, ownership, authentication, preservation, or display of works of art.

Not only have prices for art risen dramatically in the last few years, thus increasing the temptations for fraudulent and criminal activities, but whole new categories of art objects have been rescued from junk shops and attics—old photographs and decorative articles from the recent past come to mind—to enlarge the field that must be dealt with. There have been changes in the law governing gifts of art by collectors, while artists have joined in unprecedented numbers to protest a ruling that when they donate their own work they can deduct only the cost of materials—say twenty-five cents for the paper and ink used to make a print worth hundreds of dollars in the open market. That ruling, incidentally, had wide social repercussions because it not only hurt the artists, but also cut off museums, schools, and other public institutions that benefited from gifts by artists.

Meanwhile, some states have passed laws governing the sale of prints, once a negligible part of the art market but now a major field that is so complicated and so open to exploitation that the author of this book felt it necessary to make special efforts to pass the law in Illinois.

Despite the almost daily accounts of infractions of the laws involving art, it was hard, nonetheless, to get an overview of the law as it affects the business of art until attorney Scott Hodes's first book appeared. Now he has reworked and greatly enlarged that initial volume, bringing it up to date while making it valuable to a wider public.

Aside from these immediate and practical matters, the interest in legal aspects of art signals the awakening of America to the fine arts. It must be a truism that any really serious human undertaking is soon codified and then relies on law to define its scope and defend its rights. As art bulks larger in the American consciousness, it progressively loses the frivolous character our Puritan heritage gave it, and acquires dignity and honor that demand full and equal rights with other life-enhancing endeavors.

A review of the interrelations of art and the law over the centuries will show that commitments to produce art, to acquire art, to donate art, and to establish property rights in art often have led to legal action. The accounts of that action contribute extensively to our knowledge of art history. Indeed, one may assume that most major works of art become a matter of public record through legal transactions when they are commissioned and when they change ownership. And while there are some remarkable pages in the record when artist and patron, or artist and critic have clashed in court—think of Whistler and Ruskin, and some humiliating passages when blundering officials attempted ignorantly to distinguish works of fine art from mundane taxable materials—think of Brancusi's Bird in Flight *classed as metal, most of the record is sound and constructive. It provides a substantial basis for resolving present and future problems.*

One may take for granted that when millionaire dealers and patrons transact business in art their legal interests and problems are cared for adequately. One cannot safely assume as much for the artist, however, for his knowledge and resources ordinarily are meager. Too often he is the victim of his own special combination of ignorance of the law, generosity, and pride. This book is a shield for him.

The collector also needs guidance through the pitfalls of buying, importing, lending, and giving works of art, lest his innocent largesse reap troubles with tax collectors and customs officials. This book may be his salvation.

While museums may be thought of as the temples of art, well above the battles of daily life, they too are facing unprecedented problems, ranging from how to dispose of surplus art despite an alert press and vigilant donors, to picket lines and labor disputes. Museum officials have a stake in everything affecting art, from inheritance taxes to problems of security, and this book should be helpful to them.

It is a mistake to think that anything about fine art is trivial, for even nearly worthless art can be exploited, so great is popular esteem for art if not for artists. The painter or sculptor working in the studio may think of nothing but the trials and joys of creation, yet in fact he is creating his estate. Its value to him and his heirs will depend upon how clearly he understands, or even senses his rights and responsibilities. If he only senses them, probably he can find competent counsel, for I have found that the prestige and public status of art, together with highly personal and subtle matters of taste and judgment, attract the best legal minds.

Although the author has confined himself in this book to major problems arising from sales, commissions, copyright, customs, taxation, and insurance, he has regularly summarized and interpreted the law to reveal its nature and intention. Accordingly, the imaginative reader will have no difficulty in seeing beyond the usual horizons prescribed by habit and everyday experience. In a world of expanding media of communication, art remains the best all-around means of communication, internationally relevant, and so it behooves the artist and the collector of his work to look to future opportunity and hazards.

But whatever the future may bring, the present holds problems enough in which this book can prove its usefulness. The traditional stereotype of the artist who is quite incompetent in business matters belongs to the present as well as to the past. How grateful this one is to the disreputable dealer who robs him; how angry and helpless is that one who worked months on a portrait only to have it refused without payment; how stricken that other when costs of a commission ran higher than his fee! Yet a contract with the dealer, a written agreement on terms for the portrait, and a contingency clause in the commission could have prevented disaster. Too often the artist finds that he has traded his work for a puff of publicity, yet even that evanescent satisfaction can be combined with tangible rewards if the artist knows his legal rights. And should he die, leaving a valuable collection of unsold works to his family, they may lose nearly everything to estate taxes unless there is careful planning in advance.

Nor is the art collector, even when he is a business-man, likely to foresee in the specialized art world all contingencies of acquiring, protecting, and conveying to others his artistic treasures. This book can aid him, too, when dealing with the tax collector who thinks all of a painter's work must be of equal value regardless of date, or when caught in the toils of customs and import regulations. He need not learn too late of an advantageous way of giving his collection to the public, or pay for a forgery before seeking authentication, if he is alert to problems and ways of avoiding them.

Recent events have shown that even highly placed museum officials can err in the legal steps required when importing a masterpiece, with disastrous results. And the costly affair of Yale's Vinland map is further proof that the will to believe that is the mainspring of many successful frauds needs the checks and balances of legal advice.

To all such beleaguered artists, collectors, and museum people this book is addressed, and also to their more fortunate brethren whose common sense still needs legal underwriting. The book is comprehensive and imaginative enough to offer some fresh fact, insight, or suggestion to everyone. Its great charm is that it discusses the law in laymen's language, is not cluttered with references to cases, and frequently points out that some matters are so special in their circumstances and so complex in ramifications that professional legal counsel should be sought. This is not a sue-them-yourself lawbook, but is, instead, the lucid exposition by a good legal mind of common or typical problems created by conflicting interests in the field of art, together with possible remedies.

Certainly one contribution the book can make is to the education of young artists in the art schools of America. It seems scandalous to send young artists into the professional world with only the sketchiest hearsay knowledge of the ethics and business practices of art. Some schools know this and have instituted courses. All schools should require study of the legal aspects of the artist's profession, for which this book is an essential resource.

Scott Hodes, the author, a graduate of the University of Chicago, has had a personal interest in art since undergraduate days, and an exceptional opportunity to live with and abet the growth of a distinguished private art collection. His efforts here will be especially welcome by all those artists who have been striving to give status to their profession through codes of ethics, standard contract forms, and similar legal instruments, some of which are reproduced in the Appendices. Equally, collectors will applaud and benefit from information on recent government regulations as well as basic law affecting purchasing, customs, taxes, and insurance in the field of art. The new section on matters of concern to museums significantly expands the scope of the book and its usefulness, in particular, to the newer institutions in this country where, for a while, a new museum opened almost every day. Beyond this, anyone interested in the arts and their coming of age will find this valuable book both fascinating to read and instructive.

The University of Chicago
February, 1974

Harold Haydon

INTRODUCTION

This modest volume is an expanded and updated version of an earlier book written in 1966, entitled *The Law of Art and Antiques*. In these intervening eight years there has been a substantial increase in the number of works of art that have been bought and sold, both at auction and at private sale. According to press reports, large sums of money have frequently been involved in these transactions. Thus, for many, fine art now seems to be measured not only in aesthetic terms, but also in relation to economic value. These commercial overtones, by their very nature, have brought lawyers and the law to the forefront.

Many will agree that now, more than ever before, courts of law are being asked to step in and settle disputes which may involve artists, dealers, collectors, and even museums. At the same time, some states are busy enacting legislation to regulate the commercial aspects of buying and selling works of art. This is a healthy and welcome application of the law to protect those artists and collectors who are oftentimes gullible, misinformed, and easily misled.

This book explores some of the legal ramifications involved in being an artist, photographer, dealer, collector, or museum curator. This discussion is designed for the layman, but it is not intended as a guide to being your own lawyer. Rather, the book is intended to help the reader recognize when he has a legal problem and to communicate enough of the flavor of the law so that he will be able to understand and work effectively with legal counsel. The author recognizes that the law, like art itself, may elude and confuse the uninitiated. If the flavor of the law has been lost or distorted in translation, the author must take full responsibility.

PART I

THE ARTIST

Chapter 1

CREATING AND SELLING ART WORKS

I suppose that every serious artist expects to earn a decent living from his work. This is nothing to be ashamed of; an artist does not have to work in a drafty attic just to prove to the world that he is dedicated to his art. This does not mean, however, that an artist may not have to forego certain economic benefits while awaiting public acceptance. But every artist has a right, and even a duty to himself and his art to attempt to sell his creations.

For better or for worse, selling a work of art projects the artist into the realm of business and law. A sale may be consummated in a variety of ways. The artist may choose to sell his work directly to a purchaser who intends to put the object in his own home or office; he may sell through a dealer or gallery or at an art fair; he may sell a finished work, or he may produce a work to meet certain specifications or tastes. Every arrangement presents different legal problems. The purpose of this chapter is to examine types of transactions artists are likely to enter into and to warn against possible pitfalls.

COMMISSIONS TO PRODUCE

A commission is an agreement to purchase a work of art that does not yet exist, but which the artist promises to bring into being. It is generally negotiated by the artist directly with his patron. The fact that the work does not exist when the agreement is reached causes most of the legal problems an artist is likely to encounter in accepting a commission. What if his patron is not satisfied and refuses to pay?

If the patron is not to be satisfied, his pronouncement is not likely to come until the artist has almost completed his work. What happens at that point will depend on the original agreement or contract. The die was cast long before.

Operationally, a contract may be defined as an agreement, either oral or written, that will be enforced by a court of law. An oral agreement is enforceable only if it is for a period of less than one year and the amount of money involved is $500 or less. All contracts, to be enforceable, must be founded on "consideration" (something of value to be given or done in exchange for something of value to be given or done by another). The law does not ordinarily force a person to keep a promise if he does not receive something in return; the theory is that there must be an exchange to support a contract. Illustratively, a promise to paint a picture for a person is not binding unless that person promises something of value (money or the like) in return. Generally, two acts are needed to create a contract. The first is an offer, "I will give you this if you will give me that." The second is an acceptance, "Agreed."

An infinite variety of conditions or qualifications may

be made a part of any contract. "This agreement is void in the event of a strike," or "if delivery is not made within thirty days," or "if I am not satisfied with the product," are terms frequently used. Satisfaction of the patron is a clause common to many artistic commissions, and it can be a very troublesome one for the artist.

The general policy of the law is to allow people to make any kind of contract they want to, and to enforce that contract as written. This policy goes so far as to permit the making of contracts by which the duty of a party to perform his part of the bargain depends solely upon the state of his own mind—his own satisfaction. Therefore, if an artist enters a contract by the terms of which it is clear that the patron is to pay only if he is satisfied, the artist can collect only if he is able to achieve satisfaction on the part of his patron.

A person's state of mind is, of course, very hard to prove, and satisfaction is a state of mind. It is possible that a patron, having suffered a loss in the stock market, will decide that he wants to breach a contract and that he will feign dissatisfaction to avoid the appearance of a breach. It may be possible to convince a court that the dissatisfaction is feigned, but it will not be easy to do. If an artist makes this type of contract, he should be aware of the possible consequences.

Whether the artist finds himself completely at the mercy of his patron's whim may depend upon how the personal taste and satisfaction clause is written. If the contract says the artist shall be paid if he produces a "satisfactory" picture, the effect may be different than if the contract recites that the patron need pay only "if he is satisfied." Some courts may hold that a satisfactory

25

picture is one that is objectively satisfactory; that is, one that would satisfy a reasonable man. In that event, proof of quality might be made by the expert testimony of other artists or of art dealers. However, most courts will interpret satisfaction clauses to require that the product satisfy the purchaser, unless it is completely unambiguous that the standard intended was the satisfaction of a reasonable man. The assumption is made, on the basis of general observations about human nature, that satisfaction of the purchaser is probably what was intended.

When working under a personal satisfaction contract, the artist should specify that his patron pay specified portions of the contract price at various stages of the creative process. Where this is not acceptable, the artist may gain some protection by having the patron put his initials on drafts, designs, and preliminary sketches, indicating that he is satisfied at various steps of the creative process. Then should the patron show reluctance to accept the final product, there is at least some evidence available from which it may be argued that the patron's dissatisfaction is not genuine.

If a dissatisfied patron cancels his contract, the artist will usually be entitled to dispose of the work elsewhere, unless it is a mural in the patron's house, of course. A portrait, however, presents a special problem. It may be an invasion of the patron's privacy, or even a form of libel if the subject is portrayed in a derogatory light, to sell or exhibit a portrait without authorization. If a portrait just cannot be completed to the patron's satisfaction, the artist may choose to hide or destroy his work, or he may swallow his pride and renegotiate the contract at a lower price. The only other possible choice is to obtain a written release from the subject permitting exhibition or sale.

If the reader will refer back to the sample "satisfaction" clauses discussed earlier, he will note that they were so phrased that they made the patron's duty to pay contingent on satisfaction. They did not promise satisfaction. If the artist says, "I will paint a satisfactory picture in return for so much money," he has promised to satisfy. Where that is true, a failure to satisfy will be a breach of contract by the artist, though generally one with only minor consequences. Little damage has been done the patron except perhaps to waste some of his time. However, there may be fairly serious damage if the work of art is attached to the property of the patron. The patron may sustain costs in removing the unsatisfactory work, and to get what he wanted he may be required to hire another artist at a higher price. In that case, damage may be assessable to the artist if he promised to satisfy. If the work of art will be affixed to the patron's property, it is especially important for the artist to use the contingent form rather than the promissory form.

Where the work of art is a mural or becomes affixed in the house of the patron, the patron cannot retain the benefits of the artist's work, while at the same time refusing to pay. This is true even if the patron is not satisfied. There is a rule of law against unjust enrichment. In a situation of this nature, the artist is not entitled to receive his contract price because he did not fulfill his end of the bargain; however, he is entitled to a sum of money that adequately represents the value of his work. Theoretically, and as a practical matter too, the value of the artist's work should be less than the contract price since the original contract contemplated not only a work of a certain value, but one that corresponded exactly to what the patron wanted. That satisfaction should have some monetary equivalent over and above the value of the work on the open market.

DEATH OF PATRON OR ARTIST The contract between an artist and his patron is called a personal service contract. The patron is contracting for the services of a particular artist, and substitutes are not acceptable. This type of contract must be distinguished from one in which A contracts to give B's house a coat of paint. If A gets sick and cannot do the work himself, he may elect to find another painter to finish the job. B has no right to object because it makes little difference who does house painting, so long as he is reasonably competent. But a man who hires Jackson Pollack is not likely to be satisfied if he gets a Norman Rockwell. And generally, the rights and duties under a personal service contract terminate with death or disability of either party, as would be expected.

In the absence of any language to the contrary in the contract, if performance by the promisor (artist) becomes impossible by virtue of death, insanity, or disabling illness, the contract is discharged, and the artist or his estate will be under no obligation. Likewise, if the work of art is a portrait, the patron or his estate will be under no obligation if the subject, either the patron or a third person, dies before there have been any sittings. If sittings are completed, however, so that the artist can finish the painting without the subject, the patron or his estate would be liable for the agreed price. The result would probably be different if the artist had promised to "satisfy" the person who died. In this case, the contract would most likely be discharged for failure of consideration.

The rules discussed in this section are those that would be applied where the contract makes no provision for a contingency such as death, because that contingency was not contemplated when they entered the contract. Courts have rules, based on common sense, to help them guess what the parties to a contract would have wanted in a specific situation had they foreseen that such a situation might arise. Probably the main function of an attorney in the writing of a contract is to help his client to explore possibilities that would not ordinarily occur to the client, to advise the client to decide in advance how these possibilities should be dealt with, and to express the client's position in a manner that will be both clear and legally binding. When that is done, questions are less likely to arise in the first place; and when they do, courts will not have to guess the intentions of the parties. Of course, the parties to a contract may decide to do exactly the opposite of what a court, shooting in the dark, would guess they would want done. As long as the result is not illegal or against public policy, the courts will go along. After all, one of the main doctrines of contract law is that the parties should be free to contract as they choose.

PRODUCING "ORIGINAL" PRINTS

There has always been a premium on originality. In the case of a painting or a drawing, there is only the one original, whereas in the case of a print, there may be many originals. The originality of a print implies that the work was designed and executed by one and the same person. Nevertheless, there is considerable authority for the proposition that the artist may permit a professional printmaker to complete the process under his supervision without destroying originality.

To the serious artist the proliferation of reproductions made by photochemical and other processes poses a real problem. Reproductions, which are usually produced in unlimited numbers, may sometimes be palmed off as original prints (lithographs, seriographs, etchings, woodcuts). By contrast, original prints are issued in limited editions, each print generally being numbered and signed by the artist.

Since novice collectors are many and frequently moneyed, it is not surprising that sharp business practices have arisen in marketing "original" prints. Surely no art buyer would wish to pay a premium for an original print only to discover that he has acquired a photochemical reproduction of inferior value. A seller who represents a reproduction to be an original has committed a fraud (see page 113).

In order to insure the integrity of his work, the artist should inspect each print and approve it if it meets his criteria of originality and quality. He should then sign the print and number it. His signature will become a guaranty of authenticity and originality for prospective buyers.

Today most artists employ professional printmakers. This may be due to the fact that a good printing press or plate-making equipment is bulky and would take up a great deal of space in the artist's studio. Probably the real reason, however, is that quality in printing is dependent upon manual manipulation and technical expertise. This is especially true in lithography. Because of the printer's close relationship with the artist, it is advisable for the artist to memorialize his arrangement in a contract.

A contract between an artist and his printmaker should, among other things, reserve the artist's right to approve the final prints and affix his signature to each. It is important, too, that the printmaker agrees to efface the stones or plates upon the completion of the edition. This will preclude overruns on the first edition, restrikes from the original plate, and reprinting another edition on a different kind of paper. By taking these precautions, the artist will insure that reproductions are not later represented as "original" prints.

The contract with the printmaker should also provide that the print be registered for copyright in the artist's name in the United States Copyright Office, with the necessary copyright notation on each print. Other matters that should be covered in the contract include the number of prints that will comprise the edition and the contemplated retail selling price. The compensation arrangement between the artist and the printmaker should also be included in the contract since the parties' memory or a handshake may later lead to differences of opinion. (See Appendix I, Agreement with a Printmaker.)

SALES BY A PHOTOGRAPHER

While some artists are recording their impressions on canvas or in clay, others are expressing their feelings through photography. A photograph, like a painting, not only can express the way things really are, but also can express the creator's feelings about them. Too often, however, creative people in the field of photography are not considered to be artists. This is unfair and unrealistic.

The photographer is exposed to many of the same legal problems as the painter or sculptor, and the materials included in this book should be read by the photographer with this point in mind. Some of these problems may arise because photographers, like other artists, do not customarily enter into elaborate agreements. This neglect could be costly, especially where a right to reproduce or a copyright is involved.

There are, however, some problems unique to the photographer. At the very outset, many photographers deliver their film to processors and receive a simple receipt in return. This generally occurs without the realization that most receipts contain a legend limiting the processors' liability for loss or damage to the cost of replacing the film. Unfortunately, the first time most photographers realize that their receipts contain this limitation is when the film is actually lost or damaged. Since most receipts are not signed by the photographer, the receipt itself cannot be considered a contract and the photographer is not bound by its specific terms and conditions. If, however, the processor specifically notifies the photographer that its liability is to be limited, the photographer may have implicitly accepted this limitation by depositing his film under these circumstances. But proving that the photographer had knowledge is not always easy, and courts of law will most likely place the burden of such proof on the processors.

The photographer may also encounter legal difficulties in selling his work. Where a photograph is sold outright, the buyer is paying for all of the rights inherent in the photograph as well as the absolute right to deal with the photograph. The buyer will even acquire the right to crop or retitle the photograph. In addition, the buyer is entitled to receive certain assurances. These include warranties by the photographer that he created and owns the photograph, that the photograph is original, that the photograph does not infringe on any right of a third party, and that the photograph has not heretofore been published or promised for publication. As further protection, the buyer may ask the photographer to obtain written right of privacy releases from all persons depicted in the photograph.

The photographer, like the artist engaged in making prints, should determine in advance the size of the edition. Moreover, each print in the edition should be signed and numbered by the photographer. The photographer should also make sure that the number of pictures in the edition is not increased. As in the case of "original" prints, the size of the edition will ultimately become an important factor in determining value. It is, therefore, recommended that the photographer or the printmaker retire the negative by punching a hole in it. Some photographers even go to the trouble of punching the word "cancelled" on the negative.

If a photograph is not being sold outright, the photographer should list specifically what rights he is granting and should state that all other rights belong to him. These rights involve the extent to which the reproduction of his photograph will be permitted. For example, a photographer may convey, among other rights, a "one-time" right, a "first" right, an "exclusive" right, a "distribution" right, or a "promotion" right, or a combination of these rights. If a "one-time" right is granted, the purchaser can reproduce the photograph once in one language, of one edition, of one publication, in a predetermined area. If, instead, a "first" right is granted, the purchaser will acquire a prior right to publish the photograph for a predetermined period of time. Where an "exclusive" right is involved, the purchaser will obtain the complete authority to reproduce the photograph for an unlimited period of time. Other rights, of course, can be granted, such as a right to reproduce a photograph in a publication for "distribution" in a certain area; or a right to use the photograph in the "promotion" or advertising of a publication. In any case, it is important for the photographer to define exactly what rights he is granting to a purchaser. Although further protection from unauthorized use is available under the Copyright Law, a definitive agreement is preferable.

Where photographs or transparencies are tendered for approval to a prospective purchaser, the photographer should exercise great care to spell out the terms of submission. At the outset, it is advisable to state that the photographs shall, at all times, remain the property of the photographer and shall be returned promptly after being used. It is also important to specify that the purchaser shall be held responsible for loss or damage to the photographs from the time of receipt until the time of their return. Moreover, the parties should agree in advance to the value of each transparency in the event that it is later lost or damaged. If a photographer takes these precautionary measures he should be able to avoid a later controversy with the purchaser.

SALE THROUGH A DEALER OR GALLERY

Probably the most popular method of selling art is to locate a dealer who will undertake to publicize and sell the artist's works. The dealer generally sells through gallery showings or exhibitions. In this way, art critics and the public are given an opportunity to see, evaluate, and purchase the artist's works.

The artist and the art dealer may enter into one of two general arrangements, either of which may be varied in an infinite number of details. Basically, the dealer may purchase art and resell it, or serve as the artist's agent, selling on a commission or fee basis works that are owned, until sale, by the artist. As an example of variations within these two general classes, when the dealer buys he may agree to buy and the artist to sell, the artist's entire output; the dealer may take a certain specified portion; he may have a right of first refusal; or he may just buy an occasional work. Where the dealer contracts to purchase all of the artist's output, the artist is bound by law to sell to the dealer every work he produces. Where the dealer has the right of first refusal only, if the dealer decides not to purchase, the artist is free to sell to a third party.

If the works continue to belong to the artist while in the hands of the dealer, the dealer is serving as an agent for the artist. In this situation an artist should negotiate a consignment sales agreement so that the artist retains ownership of his works until he has been paid by the dealer, and is protected from the dealer's creditors in the event the dealer goes bankrupt. (See discussion of New York statute below and Appendix II for a Consignment Sale Form that reserves a security interest for the artist's benefit.)

New York has enacted a statute regulating the artist-dealer relationship in an effort to protect the artist from some of the problems that can result from failure to memorialize the business arrangement. Under the statute, when a dealer accepts an artist's work to sell or exhibit in return for a commission or other compensation, the dealer's acceptance is deemed to be on consignment; that is, the artist (consignor) retains superior right, title, and interest to the art works. This is especially important if the dealer should suffer bankruptcy, in which case the artist's works are free from the claims of the dealer's creditors. The works of art and proceeds from their sale are considered trust property to be held by the dealer for the artist's benefit. When a dealer purchases works of art for his own account, which were initially received on consignment, they remain trust property until the artist is paid in full. If a dealer resells this trust property before completing payment to the artist, the proceeds of that resale are trust funds held for the artist to the extent necessary to pay any balance still owed. The statute also has waiver provisions, drafted to the artist's advantage, limiting which parts of the statute can be waived by the artist and clearly specifying the substance of a waiver.

In law, an agent has certain well-defined responsibilities. His fundamental role is to act on behalf of his principal, usually for certain limited and specified purposes.

36

For example, an agent empowered to sell an artist's works would not also have the power to sell the artist's house. But the agent does have the power, as long as the agency relationship exists, to sell a painting or a sculpture, and the artist cannot interfere when the agent has contracted with a third party to sell one of the artist's works. The artist cannot come in and say, "I don't think you charged enough money for that piece," or "I've decided to keep that painting." In the absence of an agreement to the contrary, the agent (gallery) may bind the principal (artist) to any deal within the scope of the agent's authority.

An artist and a dealer may enter into an agency relationship by a formal, written contract, or by very informal means. For example, an artist may create an agency by leaving his work with the dealer, and it will be assumed that the artist consents to be bound by the contractual arrangements that are normally given by this dealer. Then, too, an agency to procure commission agreements for the artist may arise informally as the result of a stranger indicating that he knows a person who would like to commission the artist. If the artist accepts the commission, he will probably be bound to compensate the volunteer agent at a reasonable rate. Whether the artist leaves his work with the dealer or accepts a commission negotiated by a volunteer agent, the agency relationship, even though informal, may be a continuing one until definite steps are taken to terminate it. Basically, then, it is the artist as principal who is responsible for the creation of the agency relationship. Therefore, if the artist chooses to end the relationship, he must so advise the agent and also serve notice to the public, so that persons who may deal with the agent will not be misled.

The law recognizes that a dealer has certain fiduciary responsibilities toward the artist. The dealer must remain within the scope of the authority granted to him by the artist. If the artist has specified that certain pieces within the possession of the dealer are not for sale, the dealer must not violate this trust. The dealer cannot purposely sell the artist's work at a cut-rate price to his friends. Likewise, if the dealer fails to exert care for the artist's works that are in his possession, he may be held liable for their market value in the event of loss or damage. If expensive or rare works of art are involved, the artist should consider insurance against loss or damage not resulting from dealer lack of care. (Insurance of art works is discussed in detail on pages 161 to 170.) Moreover, if the artist has given the dealer an exclusive agency agreement, the dealer must exercise reasonable efforts to publicize and sell the artist's work. Regardless of the type of contract that is negotiated between the artist and the dealer, the artist is not bound to perform unless and until the agent actually exerts some substantial effort on the artist's behalf.

Written contracts have certain advantages over informal agreements. By negotiating and committing the terms of an agency relationship to writing, each of the parties will avoid many of the difficulties that may arise in the future. Obviously, it is better for the parties to have decided in advance how contingencies are to be handled than to leave the question to judicial interpretation in a lawsuit. The failure to negotiate a binding contract at the inception of a working relationship has destroyed countless friendships and has consumed untold sums in legal fees and court costs. The contracts entered into between Henri Matisse and his dealer should be examined carefully as they exhibit considerable ingenuity in solving problems that may well have arisen had Matisse merely left his paintings with a dealer and said, "Please sell them for me." These contracts are reproduced in Appendix III. For comparative purposes, a recent Artist-Dealer Form of Contract distributed by the Artists Equity Association is reproduced in Appendix IV.

ACCOUNTING AND RECORDS Upon entering into a dealer relationship or gallery sales agreement, an artist should negotiate a written agreement regulating record keeping and accounting practices. Many galleries and dealers either fail to keep adequate records or maintain them in a form upon which the artist cannot rely. This situation, in turn, may result in missing or unaccounted-for art works and even create a situation where the artist is unable to trace a work of art after sale. Inadequate or incomprehensible records may even deprive the artist of the opportunity to determine whether he is receiving a fair compensation for his works. For in many artist-dealer arrangements the artist agrees upon a minimum sale price for each work and lets the dealer determine the actual sale price. Inadequate record keeping would encourage an unscrupulous dealer to quote fictitious low sales prices to the artist and to pocket the excess. The greatest drawback for the artist, however, is that without the benefit of a proper accounting, the artist will find himself in a weak bargaining position in the event the minimum price becomes an issue.

The artist should demand that the dealer or gallery maintain a separate inventory of his works and allow periodic access for inspection of these records. If installment sales are made, the artist should be given a periodic accounting of the payment status of each work. The artist should receive sales receipt copies for any work sold, reflecting the sale price and the dealer's or gallery's commission or compensation. The sales receipt should also recite pertinent information on the buyer which might aid in resolving any future authentication questions. An artist must, for his protection, have his own records. Not only are such records essential for income tax purposes, but they can be used to verify those maintained by the gallery or dealer. A simple records system could consist of a large index card with a photograph of the work attached, notations of useful data made on the card, and any receipts or documents clipped to the back.

SALE THROUGH ART RENTAL OUTLETS

It has been estimated that there are approximately five hundred art collectors throughout the world who comprise the market for high-priced objects of art— those works priced at $50,000 or more. While the purchases and sales of these recognized individual art buyers make spectacular news, the art market does not exist on these transactions. As a matter of fact, the art market is not designed for these buyers. The average buyer is probably interested in works that sell for less than $300.

40

In an effort to penetrate the real art market and assist the up-and-coming artist, a museum or gallery will frequently offer an art rental service to its patrons. This service permits the artist to display works of art in the hope that a collector will rent, and eventually purchase, his work. (Legal problems confronting the collector in this situation are discussed on pages 127 to 128.)

Most contracts entered into between an art rental agency and an artist stipulate that the artist shall set the selling price and that the rental agency is entitled to a specified commission or handling charge for its services. Frequently too, the artist agrees to transport his works to and from the art rental outlet, and assumes responsibility for any loss or damage that may occur in transit. Another provision may recite that the articles will not be cleaned or repaired either by the art rental service or by the borrower, except with the written permission of the artist. Most rental services also agree to insure all items in their possession, with the understanding that potential liability will not exceed the selling price. As a measure to protect his copyright, the artist should insist that the agreement between the art rental outlet and the borrower specify that works of art will not be photographed, sketched, or otherwise reproduced without the express written consent of the artist.

Any agreement between the artist and rental agency should necessarily provide for termination of the relationship. This is generally effected by written notice from one party to the other. At the time of notification, the artist's works should be removed promptly from the rental agency, unless they are on loan at that time. In this event, the artist should wait until the article is returned by the borrower. Should the borrower exercise his option to purchase the work after the artist-agency agreement is terminated, but before the termination of the lease, the artist may not be entitled to the return of the article.

Over the past ten years, many art museums throughout the United States have opened art rental outlets. This vehicle has enabled the contemporary artist to expose the public to his works. It is of the utmost importance that the artist exercise great care when entering into a relationship with a rental agency; when doubtful about any provisions of their agreement, he is best advised to seek the assistance of a competent attorney. (See Appendix V for a sample Agreement between the Artist and an Art Rental Outlet.)

SALES AT ART FAIRS

Art fairs, with their festive atmospheres, provide an opportunity for many artists to exhibit and sell their works directly to buyers on a "cash and carry" basis, thus eliminating many of the problems and some of the expense inherent in dealing through a dealer or a middleman. For the most part, artists exhibiting at art fairs are either amateurs or those who are not recognized as "established." (See Purchasing from the Artist at page 128.) But then most buyers are not sophisticated art collectors looking for "Rembrandts," but are individuals who are looking for a decorative work at a price they can or wish to pay. The combination of many artists with many different styles and many buyers with divergent tastes often results in both parties being satisfied at an art fair.

In spite of the informality of an art fair, the artist should recognize that an unrestricted sale of an art work will transfer all right, title, and interest to the purchaser. Should an artist wish to restrict the reproduction, alteration or use of his work, he should copyright the work and execute a sales contract with the buyer that specifically reserves the copyright to the artist. (A discussion of copyrights is on pages 47 to 74, and a sample Agreement for the Sale of Painting, with Reservation of Copyright, is in Appendix VI.) Further, if an artist has an exclusive sales arrangement with a dealer or gallery, a sale by him at a fair will constitute a breach of contract and expose him to the possibility of a lawsuit for damages.

The absence of a dealer or middleman does not alleviate the necessity of adequate record-keeping on the part of the artist. The artist should retain information relating to the buyer in the event a question of authentication or copyright should arise. Good records are also invaluable and very necessary in the preparation of the artist's income tax and the payment of sales tax in those states imposing a tax. Also, some expenses incurred in producing and selling art work are tax deductible, but may be very difficult to substantiate without records in the event of an audit by the Internal Revenue Service. (See the Artist and Taxes on pages 89 to 106.)

DOING BUSINESS AS A CORPORATION

Monumental sculpture, ranging from large, floating mobiles to huge buildings wrapped in fabric (for example, Christo's wrapping of the Museum of Contemporary Arts in Chicago), is characteristic of modern art. Unfortunately, in some cases, artists creating such works of art may, by the sheer size and design of their projects, endanger the lives of persons or the integrity of property. If damage should occur or if a person is killed or injured, all of the artist's personal assets may be subjected to a lawsuit by the injured party.

There really is no ideal form for doing business that will be best for every situation involving risk. However, doing business as a corporation should be considered by an artist who is embarking on a venture that has significant potential dangers both to persons and to property. Incorporation will limit the artist's financial exposure since he will not be liable for any more money than the amount he has put into his corporation. His house and his personal assets will be free from attack by creditors in the event that damage or injury does occur. Sometimes this potential risk may be covered by insurance, but frequently the premiums for insurance of this nature are beyond the artist's financial means.

Although limiting liability is an important consideration, corporations have other legal attributes as well. These include, among others, the continuation of a business after the death of an owner, the control of the business by a few people, and the free transferability of corporate shares. There are also special tax considerations which may be involved, and these are discussed briefly on pages 98 to 99. All of these factors should be carefully weighed by persons entering business, in addition to consulting a competent attorney.

MEDIATION AND ARBITRATION

When an artist and his patron or an artist and his dealer develop a dispute, a third party may be asked to lend his good offices to help solve the problem. This is known as mediation and it in no way binds the respective parties. On the other hand, a dispute may be referred to a third party by mutual agreement of the parties, made either prior to the actual dispute in anticipation of foreseeable difficulty, or after the dispute has arisen. This type of an agreement, known as arbitration, will usually make the decision of the third party binding on the disputants.

When parties wish to have possible disputes settled by arbitration, they may use the services of the American Arbitration Association. The association maintains panels in more than thirteen hundred cities, and for a nominal fee will supply a panel consisting of two or three association members, frequently specialists in the field of dispute. The panel will generally conduct an informal hearing before handing down a decision.

CODES OF ETHICS

In an effort to bring order out of chaos in the field of art merchandising, codes of ethics have been adopted for the professional artist and for the commercial buyer of art work by various associations and guilds. For the most part, these standards are predicated upon the belief that adherence to a code of fair practice will contribute to the welfare of the artist by establishing and building professional and public respect. The Code of Ethics of the Artists Equity Association is reproduced in Appendix VII and the Code of Fair Practice as formulated by the Joint Ethics Committee of the Society of Illustrators, the Art Directors Club, the Artists Guild, and the ASMP—the Society of Photographers in Communications, Inc.—is reproduced in Appendix VIII. These codes are modified from time to time by formal amendment or as a result of interpretation in hearings before the bodies that administer these codes.

Chapter 2

COPYRIGHT

An artist, writer, or painter is a social being, and art is a form of communication. The author is probably as much flattered by the number of people who read his book as he is at the size of his royalty check. Likewise, the painter or sculptor whose work is thought worthy of acquisition for public display may receive greater satisfaction from this accomplishment than if the work is acquired by a private collector who alone will receive his message. Some artists, even in this commercial age, will waive any payment for works of art which they may create for public institutions.

Because art is in part a public activity, a myriad of legal problems may arise. As a general rule, the artist does not wish to restrict the legitimate publicity given his talents through photographs, sketches, reproductions, and the like. Yet, the artist properly concerned with earning a livelihood from his work, must protect himself from publicity given for purposes of economic exploitation. How can the artist expose his works to the public, while reserving for himself alone, the rights pertaining to those works? This is the problem that has led to copyright legislation.

HISTORY OF COPYRIGHT LEGISLATION

Long before the War of Independence, it had been established by the common, or judge-made, law of England that the creator of an intellectual work owned that work just as he did the chair upon which he sat. This ownership or property right, which prevented copying as well as stealing, continued as long as the creator did not expose his work to the public. What rights he had after exposure or publication were, at best, open to question until the enactment of the first copyright legislation in 1710, the Statute of Anne. That statute, upon which all subsequent copyright legislation is based, was enacted in response to pressure from the printing industry, not too long after restrictions on entering the printing business had been lifted. With anyone able to open a printing establishment, there was always the temptation to pirate a competitor's best seller.

The old common law copyright continued to exist even in the presence of a statute, but only until such time as publication was effected. The statutory copyright was available to the creator only after his work was published. This distinction continues in American law. We now have federal copyright legislation applicable once a work has been published, and common law rights, administered by the individual states, respecting works that are still in the possession of their creators.

The modern American copyright law, like the Statute of Anne, gives the owner of the copyright a monopoly to reproduce his work for a period of years. Prevailing American law protects that right for twenty-eight years after the first publication, with the provision that a copyright can be renewed for a second twenty-eight year period. As long as a work remains unpublished, however, the copyright has no time limitation and the property rights in the work may be passed on for generations without losing its common law copyright.

WHAT CAN BE COPYRIGHTED

The power of Congress to enact uniform copyright (and patent) laws was granted by the United States Constitution. Original copyright laws were concerned only with written works, so the Constitution (Article 1, Section 8, Clause 8) provided that "the Congress shall have the power . . . to promote the Progress of Science and useful Arts, by securing for limited Times to Authors and Inventors the exclusive Right to their respective Writings and Discoveries." In implementing this grant of power, Congress rejected the idea of subsidies or patronage as a stimulus to the arts. Instead, economic incentive for our creative citizens was provided in the form of the legal protection accorded by a copyright.

Over the years, the terms *author* and *writing*, as used in the Constitution, were interpreted by the courts of law to include musicians and their music and graphic artists and their works. And before an author could be given a copyright, he had to reduce his work to a writing. A musician likewise had to produce sheet music or a recording, and a graphic artist either the work itself or a model from which it could be produced. The copyright law does not protect a mere idea which has not been reduced to some tangible form of expression.

The Copyright Law (Title 17, United States Code) lists fourteen classes of copyrightable works, but adds that these "specifications" shall not "limit the subject matter of copyright." Although the law provides that "all writings of an author" are eligible for copyright protection, the courts have indicated that certain types of works, which may constitute "writings" in the constitutional sense, do not come within the present scope of the copyright law. As a rule of thumb, a work must fit into one of the fourteen categories specified in the statute in order to qualify for statutory protection.

In addition, because the word "author" is defined as "one who originates or creates," courts have inferred a requirement that there be originality in order to obtain a copyright. Originality in this context merely means that a work must be independently created by its author. The work need not be strikingly unique or novel to be copyrighted. It is sufficient if it is a distinguishable variation of a prior work. It cannot be a mere copy.

Of particular interest to the artist is Class G and Class H of the Copyright Law. Class G includes works of the fine arts and works of artistic craftsmanship, insofar as their form, but not their mechanical or utilitarian aspects are concerned. Paintings, drawings, sculpture, and the like are included in this category. (See Form G Application for Registration of a Claim to Copyright in a work of art or model or design for a work of art in Appendix IX). Class H generally covers reproductions of existing works of art in the same or different media. Reproductions of paintings, sculpture, or other works of art in the forms of etchings, drawings, and lithographs are included in this class. (See Form H Application for Registration of a Claim to Copyright in a reproduction of a work of art in Appendix X.)

Although the question of originality is rarely raised with respect to painters and sculptors, it may appear to present a problem for photographers. Yet in the words of one famous judge, "No photograph, however simple, can be unaffected by the personal influence of the author. . . ." Consequently, by virtue of the choice of subject matter, angle, lighting, kind of lens, and other factors, a photograph will ordinarily be found to exhibit sufficient originality to be eligible for protection under the Copyright Law. Yet many photographers unknowingly fail to copyright their works, thereby permitting their handiwork to fall into the public domain. Class J of the Copyright Law covers photographic prints and filmstrips, slide films, and individual slides and permits registration prior to publication on Form J (Appendix XI). On the other hand, reproductions of photographs prepared by photolithography, photoengraving, and other mechanical processes (such as greeting cards and picture postcards) are generally regarded as "prints" rather than "photographs" and, after publication, should be submitted for registration on Form K (Appendix XII). In some cases a photograph is first published in a periodical. Where this occurs the photographer should request that a separate copyright notice appear accompanying his photograph. This will be considered as a "contribution to a periodical" and should be registered on Form BB.

The development of new art forms has raised interesting and sometimes puzzling questions of copyright. For example, are the remains of the artist's dinner found in chance positions on tables, in boxes, or elsewhere a copyrightable work of art if objects are fixed or frozen as they lie and then turned vertically and hung on a wall [Marcel Duchamp's *Dinner* (1964)]? Or is a decorated taxi inside of which a complicated system of tubing produces a localized rainstorm that drenches a dummy driver and passenger a work of art that may be copyrighted [Salvador Dali's *Rainy Taxi* (1938)]? It is

51

obvious that these unique forms of art stretch the traditional forms of copyrightable material to their limits.

COPYRIGHT OR PATENT Since confusion may develop over whether a work is subject to a copyright or a patent, it may be advisable to differentiate between the two forms of protection. A *copyright* protects intellectual creations in the form of literary, dramatic, musical, or artistic works, while a *patent* protects inventions in the form of mechanical devices, processes, and the like. A copyright would protect the design of a piece of jewelry, but it would not protect the clasp. It has been held that a statuette mass-produced as a lamp base can be copyrighted. Neither the fact that the figure was associated with a utilitarian object nor that it was mass-produced removed this object from the copyrightable category. However, a design for a utilitarian object (for example, a housing for a mixmaster) would be protected under patent rather than copyright laws.

Although the distinction between these two forms of protection is obvious in most cases, questions may arise where the artist is eligible for a design patent. This type of patent has a maximum term of fourteen years and is given for "any new, original and ornamental design for an article of manufacture." Historically, an artist-inventor could not apply for protection under both the copyright and design patent acts, and was forced to make an election. In a recent case, however, involving a novelty watch face depicting a caricatured political personality, the court decided that there is an area of overlap where a certain type of creation may be the subject matter of both a copyright and a design patent.

As a result, the artist-inventor may receive protection against the copying of his work of art as well as the right to exclude others from making, using or selling his invention.

Nevertheless, most serious artists, because they are not creating a design for a mass-produced item, will be concerned only with copyright protection. What is protected by a copyright is the manner of expressing an idea, not the idea or subject itself. A copyright precludes anyone from imitating the artist's painting of the Eiffel Tower or a Campbell soup can, but it does not prevent someone else from making his own painting of the same subject matter, even from the same point of view. In other words, it is intentional copying, not accidental duplication, that is prohibited. Consequently, no one checks before issuing copyright papers to determine whether or not the applicant appears to have duplicated the subject of some earlier work; a patent is given only after the Patent Office has searched the records of existing patents and concluded that the invention is both novel and utilitarian.

WHO CAN SECURE A COPYRIGHT

If an object is copyrightable, the question then arises who can secure and hold a copyright? As previously discussed, the rights bestowed by copyright legislation merely replace and legally secure those postpublication rights the creator enjoyed under the common law. The postpublication rights were actually an extension of the common law prepublication rights, which are still in existence.

According to the common law, the right to control the

reproduction of unpublished works belonged exclusively to the creator. It is only when an artist does work for another, either as an employee or by accepting a commission, that the common law, prepublication copyright belongs to another and may be converted without the consent of the creator into a statutory, postpublication copyright. Therefore, where a work can be shown to have been made for hire, the employer is given all property rights in the very first instance, whether or not he had anything to do with the creation of the work, and the creator's rights are limited to those that may be specified in his employment contract.

It is generally accepted that the copyright follows the work of art even where the art work was created without a specific purchaser in mind. This may be varied by contractual agreement. The artist can agree to transfer a picture to his client, while reserving for himself all rights to reproduce the picture (see Appendix VI for a sample agreement reserving a copyright). In this case, the client receives a tangible object, the painting, stripped of all reproduction rights. Any agreement of this type should include a provision allowing the artist to gain reasonable access to the art work, so that he can reproduce it.

A copyright is considered a transferable piece of property which may accompany, or be separated from the original work from which it came into being. A copyright is also regarded as a divisible piece of property, which may be transferred in whole or in part. The holder of a copyright may license a printer to publish in a certain country or in a specified medium, while reserving for himself the right to publish in other localities or in other forms. Likewise, when the owner of a copyright dies, the property right devolves in accordance with the testator's will, or by the laws of succession when there is no will.

If there is no written agreement to the contrary, the sale of a work of art, prior to publication, carries with it the common law copyright. The artist should be aware of this when he sells his work. If, on the other hand, the work has been published (made so widely public that a court would consider it a part of the public domain), the common law copyright will have been destroyed and the purchaser will only receive a tangible art work without any copyright privileges. In this situation the purchaser cannot perfect a statutory copyright since the common law copyright would not pass with the sale of the object.

Frequently, photographers, unlike painters and sculptors, expose their works in a newspaper or magazine without taking the time to secure a copyright. Instead they choose to rely on the protection of the copyright notice in the periodical itself. This is a risky practice since photographers often grant only "one time" rights, or otherwise restrict the rights of the periodical. In this situation the copyright notice for the magazine or newspaper may not protect the photograph. If, however, the photographer sells the work outright, the copyright notice in the periodical is sufficient protection. When this latter procedure is followed, the photographer should ask for an agreement in advance that the periodical will assign the copyright back to the photographer after it is published. As a final measure, the photographer should record this assignment in the Copyright Office.

It is noteworthy that New York has enacted a statute that provides that an artist who does not copyright his work retains all reproduction rights, unless he expressly grants them away. However, it appears that this statute would only apply in those situations where the sale or exhibition of the work did not constitute a publication. Regardless of this statutory protection, the artist would be more secure if he complied with the federal copyright notice requirements.

LEGAL PROTECTION OFFERED BY COPYRIGHT

If a work of art is reproduced in violation of a statutory copyright, the copyright holder has recourse to a number of different legal remedies. Each of the following may be requested individually or cumulatively: (1) injunctive relief; (2) either the actual damages suffered by the copyright owner together with profits made by the infringer, or statutory damages; and (3) the right to have the infringing material impounded by the court. As a final measure of relief, the court may, in its discretion, compel the infringer to pay court costs and reasonable attorney's fees expended by the owner of the copyright.

The remedies discussed above are those available when an infringement of a statutory copyright has occurred. When a common law (prepublication) copyright is infringed, the remedies would be those provided by the laws of each individual state. The remedies available under state law would be much the same as those for infringement of the federal statutory copyright, except that the rules for determining the measure of damages would be inapplicable and the remedy which permits the destruction of plates or copies might not be available.

WHAT CONSTITUTES AN INFRINGEMENT

It should be evident from our previous discussion that for there to be an "infringement" there must be an actual copying or reproducing of a copy. A photographer's right in his copyrighted picture is not infringed if another person photographs the same subject. And where the question at issue concerns a copyrighted reproduction of an art work already in the public domain, the slightest difference between original and subsequent reproductions is likely to be sufficient to absolve the second publisher from a charge of copying the reproduction. On the other hand, were a person to discover and prepare a catalogue of the unpublished works of an artist, it is likely that he would be found in violation of the common law copyright. It would be presumed, were an effort to catalogue undertaken, that it was economically advantageous to the publisher, and that the artist's works were being unlawfully appropriated without just compensation.

An infringement may, therefore, be a use of the whole work or a use of some distinguishable part of the whole (if that small part of the work would normally be included in a catalogue by itself). However, one may infringe by copying the bulk of a work with only such minor differences as might be included to avoid the appearance of having copied. An infringement in the field of visual arts would undoubtedly become a close question of fact. There has been little or no litigation in this area.

The courts do not want to foreclose a popular theme (soup cans, for instance) by granting to the first person who paints the subject a right to prohibit anyone else from doing so. On the other hand, the courts cannot allow the inept copyist to escape the penalties for infringement by virtue of his inability to copy exactly, or the plagiarist to escape by creating small intentional differences. Courts must examine the facts in each case to decide if an infringement has occurred.

The question of infringement may arise in the context of a parody. A parody is a humorous imitation of a serious artistic creation, and to be a recognizable parody, the imitator must rely on certain elements of the original work, which are recognized as such. It has been held, over much criticism, that a parody by Jack Benny of a movie took so many elements of the original as to become an infringement. The defense, of course, claimed that Jack Benny, a recognized humorist, should have a right to comment upon the artistic works of another. Nevertheless, in view of this decision, the courts are likely to find an infringement in situations where the borrowing is very extensive and liberal, and where the parody is undertaken primarily with a view toward profit rather than toward meaningful criticism.

FAIR USE This raises the question of the "fair use" doctrine. This concept is not even mentioned in the Copyright Statute, but has been established by the courts in an effort to avoid the unfairness that might result if the copyright owner's rights were considered absolutely exclusive. The courts have held that if the user has a valid reason to use a small portion of the copyrighted work, and if the use does not adversely affect the owner's interest, it will be treated as a "fair use" and not an infringement. It is clear that a brief quote from a book in a book review would not be an infringement. Presumably, too, the reproduction by a newspaper of a prize winner in an art competition would be a fair use, as would the publication of a picture of an art work in conjunction with a critical article. Whether reproductions in an art history, or in a biography of a painter would constitute a fair use becomes more questionable in view of a judicial decision holding that a mere cataloguing of art works is a violation of the copyright.

When quoting, copying, or reproducing, it is advisable to seek permission of the copyright holder. The Copyright Office can be helpful in tracing a copyright owner, and the Reference Division, Copyright Office, Library of Congress, Washington, D.C., will undertake a search of its records for a nominal fee. If there is any question of the applicability of the fair use doctrine for a projected use, it would be advisable to consult an attorney.

The fair use doctrine is not applicable to articles that are not under copyright, either because the article has been dedicated to the public, the copyright has expired, or the article was not subject to a statutory copyright in the first place. A copyright may be obtained on a new version of an article already in the public domain; for example, on a reproduction of an original painting, or on a revised edition of a book. The new copyright covers only the characteristics of the new version that distinguish it from the original. In fact, it is not possible to obtain any exclusive rights in the property itself when it is not protected by a copyright. For example, the annotations, introduction, and art reproductions in an edition of the Notebooks of Leonardo da Vinci, and possibly the translation as well, may be subject to copyright protection, but the Notebooks themselves are available for reprinting in an edition that does not use any of the copyrightable parts of the present edition.

There is no fair use exception for articles under common law copyright—articles that have not yet been published. A work which is not yet published is not a subject of concern to the world; it is not news, neither does the public need responsible commentary, for the work itself is not available to the public.

NONCOPYRIGHTABLE WORKS Some classes of objects are not copyrightable at all, consequently their reproduction cannot constitute a copyright infringement. These include devices for measuring or computing, such as rulers or slide rules, charts of heights and weights, calendars (though artistic reproductions associated with them may be), tables or lists that are taken from public documents and involve no creative work, formulas or systems and devices based on them, etc. Some of these classes of items may, however, be patentable.

The rule against copyrighting immoral or libelous works is a curious one. It does not prevent the author from making an effort to obtain a copyright since the Copyright Office does not examine the merits of the submitted works. Whether a work is libelous or immoral is within the domain of a court upon application by the copyright holder for an order to enjoin for an infringement. The alleged infringer can defend by charging that the work is immoral and therefore never really had an effective copyright. Presumably, a court would apply tests used in other contexts in arriving at a decision that a work of art is libelous or obscene.

60

HOW TO SECURE A COPYRIGHT

The essence of a copyright is the giving of public notice that, though an object is exposed to the public, the artist or owner of the copyright is not dedicating the work of art to the public domain. The copyright law merely provides the means for giving such notice, and if the statutory procedures are followed, the copyright owner will not surrender his rights. It is important to remember that while the Copyright Office registers claims to copyright, it does not grant a copyright.

Certain types of art work are eligible for copyright registration before they have even been published. These include works of art, musical compositions, dramas, drawings and plastic works of a scientific or technical character, photographs, motion pictures, and works prepared for oral delivery. The following types of material *cannot* be registered for copyright as unpublished works: books, prints, maps, commercial prints and labels, and reproductions of works of art. The advantages in registering works for copyright prior to publication is that the types of relief provided in the federal copyright laws may be sought if there is an unlawful infringement.

If an *unpublished* work qualifies for a statutory copyright, the applicant must register a claim in the Copyright Office. This is done by writing to the Register of Copyrights, Library of Congress, Washington, D.C., and requesting the proper application form for the type of work to be copyrighted. The applicant must then mail to the register a photograph or other identifying reproduction of the work, an application form, and a fee of $6.00. No copyright notice is required for unpublished works. If the work is later reproduced in copies and published, the law requires that a second registration be made and that all copies of the published form contain the statutory copyright notice. This procedure and the form of copyright notice to be used is the same as that followed for a published work and is outlined below.

In the case of a work that has been *published,* it is essential that all copies distributed in the United States contain the statutory copyright notice. The statutory copyright notice may consist of (1) the word "Copyright," the abbreviation "Copr.," or the symbol "©," (2) the name of the claimant, and (3) the year of first publication (although this is normally not required); for example:

Copyright (or *Copr.* or ©) *Fred Roe* 1962.

In order not to deface certain graphic works, an alternative notice is available. It consists of the symbol "©" accompanied by the initials, monogram, or mark of the copyright owner, but the owner's name must appear on some accessible part of the work. If the symbol "©" is used the copyright may gain international protection as well (see discussion of International Copyright on pages 72 to 73). The problem of providing adequate notice can, at times, be difficult.

In a recent case where a copyright notice was placed upon a statue in such a manner as to be unobservable by a person standing on the ground, the court held that sufficient notice had not been given. Where a photograph is to be mounted, framed, or displayed in such a way that the copyright notice on the rear is inaccessible or invisible, the copyright notice should also be placed on the front of the photograph. A troublesome question may arise if the art work is a repetitive design on wallpaper or cloth. Is it appropriate to place the copyright symbol or mark on the selvage of wallpaper, which may be covered up once the wallpaper is applied? Aside from a few unusual situations that may be encountered, the mere giving of notice in the statutory form on all copies is sufficient as a first step in securing a statutory copyright.

After affixing proper notice to the object, the second step is to deposit "promptly" with the Register of Copyrights two complete copies of "the best edition then published" along with a registration form and the statutory fee of $6.00. Where the work to be copyrighted has not been reproduced but is an original plastic or graphic work, one photograph may be submitted in lieu of the two copies. If the work is later reproduced, two copies of the reproduction must be submitted. Upon proper registration, the Register of Copyrights will issue a certificate which will serve as prima facie evidence of all the facts stated thereon. Should the claimant fail to submit copies after publication, and after a demand from the register, a fine may be levied and copyright protection will be lost. However, the mere failure to submit a copy or copies to the register will not preclude the copyright holder from initiating a lawsuit for infringement if, before suing, he submits the required copies.

The law provides two consecutive copyright terms, each running for twenty-eight years. The initial copyright period runs from the time of publication, not registration. For example, a work published in 1962, but not registered until 1963, would be copyrighted as of 1962.

To be entitled to the twenty-eight year extension, a work published in 1962 would have to be reregistered sometime during the year 1989. When a reproduction is made at a date subsequent to the filing of the original, the copyright year on the reproduction will be the date of the original filing, not the date of the publication of the reproduction.

It is advisable to consult an attorney if one is interested in copyrighting different versions of the same work. Improperly done, such a copyright may be ineffective and result in the loss of rights in either the original, the new version, or both.

WHEN IS A WORK PUBLISHED?

As previously mentioned, certain works are eligible for copyright only upon proper publication with notice of copyright attached. These works should be distinguished from those that may be registered in their unpublished form, but which must be reregistered at the time of publication. In either case, the artist should be aware of those acts that may constitute publication.

The reader must remember that publication operates in two ways; publication with notice is sufficient to create a statutory copyright (presuming the work is subsequently registered without difficulty), while publication without notice will result in a public dedication of the work. But how much exposure and what type of public display is sufficient to effect a statutory copyright or, on the other hand, to erase a common law copyright? Would the same degree of public exhibition that is necessary to perfect a statutory copyright be sufficient to destroy a common law copyright? The answer apparently is no!

The law seems to be that a minimal showing to the public is necessary to effect a statutory copyright, while a fairly wide showing is necessary to eliminate the common law copyright. In other words, the law looks favorably on the maintenance of these rights by making it easier to create than to destroy them.

In a well known case, the meaning of publication for purposes of a public dedication of a work of art was at issue. A painter had placed his picture on display in a gallery exhibition. Visitors paid to be admitted and, while no copyright privilege was claimed, the visitors were asked not to reproduce any of the pictures in the show. The court held that this display was not a sufficient publication to destroy the artist's common law copyright. It should be clear, however, that if notice of a copyright had been placed on the picture, the exhibition would have been a sufficient publication to perfect a statutory copyright.

As a general rule, if it is apparent that the display of a work or its exhibition is for a select group for a specific or limited purpose, the common law copyright will not be affected. For instance, if an artist circulates his work among immediate friends and critics with the understanding that the work should not be circulated or duplicated, this should not result in the loss of the common law copyright. If, on the other hand, the work is displayed so as to reasonably lead others to believe that the work is dedicated to the public, it will be so treated, regardless of the artist's true motives. In a far reaching case involving the "Chicago Picasso," the monumental work was held to have been published and to have become part of the public domain prior to its erection in

Chicago's Civic Center. The court held that the Picasso sculpture was published and entered the public domain when the maquette was published, without requisite notice, during a prepublicity campaign. The court held that the maquette was an original work that could have been copyrighted, and that the monumental sculpture itself was only a copy of the maquette.

TRANSFER OF A COPYRIGHT

The copyright statute distinguishes between ownership of the copyright and ownership of the material object that has been copyrighted. The statute further provides that the mere transfer of the material object "shall not of itself constitute a transfer of the copyright." A copyright may be assigned, granted, mortgaged, or bequeathed by will.

Since the law recognizes a difference between giving a copyright, which is termed an assignment, and merely permitting someone to use the copyright, which is known as a license, the act of transferring a copyright may have important legal consequences. For example, there may be substantially different tax consequences if a work of art is assigned, rather than licensed. Moreover, whether a particular transfer is deemed an assignment or license may also be important in deciding whether a reputed owner has the proper standing to bring a lawsuit in his own name for infringement. If the transaction takes the form of a license, the licensee must join the copyright holder in the lawsuit; when the copyright owner and the licensee are in different states there may be problems concerning the court of proper jurisdiction.

The recording section of the copyright law refers only

to "assignments," and unfortunately the dividing line between assignments and other instruments, such as exclusive licenses, mortgages, and discharges, is far from being clear. (See Appendix XIII for a sample Assignment of Copyright.) Hence, it is a wise precaution to record in the Copyright Office instruments by which the ownership of exclusive rights is transferred and in the event of litigation to leave it to a court of law to decide what type of transaction was actually involved. Unless the assignment is recorded within three months after its execution (or within six months if the transfer occurs outside the United States), the statute provides that it is "void as against any subsequent purchaser or mortgagee for a valuable consideration, without notice, whose assignment has been duly recorded." Even if the three or six month period has elapsed (as the case may be) there is still considerable value in recording an assignment since recordation is required, in any case, before the name of the new owner may be substituted in the new notice of copyright.

There is no special form for registering a transfer of interest in a copyright. Either the document itself or a notarized copy should be sent to the Register of Copyrights. (If the transfer takes place outside the United States, the transferor must acknowledge the document before a consular or legation officer who is empowered to administer oaths and act as a notary.) The Register of Copyrights will photoduplicate the document and return it to the copyright holder. The fee for registering a transfer is three dollars if the document is less than six pages in length and in respect to books, if it covers no more than one title. If the document is longer, or if more than one title of a book is involved, there is an additional charge of fifty cents per page or per extra title. The appropriate sum should accompany the document when mailed to the register.

PROTECTION OF TITLES

The artist cannot copyright the title of his work, only the work of art itself. However, a court may protect the title under certain circumstances by applying the theory of unfair competition. The theory behind guarding against unfair competition is that the user should not be permitted to capitalize on the efforts of another and to deceive the public. In those cases where a title has acquired an "everyday" meaning, courts will be sympathetic to the original user. Generally the courts apply the following tests to determine if the title has acquired an "everyday" meaning: (1) the extent of its advertising and popularization; (2) the period of time that the title has been used, and (3) the public reaction over a period of time to the title. It should be emphasized that the mere adoption of a title does not give it protection, but once the title has gained an "everyday" meaning it may be protected (if there is a likelihood of deception or confusion) against even innocent usage by another. (The theory of Unfair Competition is discussed in greater detail on pages 83 to 84.)

THE MORAL RIGHT DOCTRINE

The moral right doctrine ("droit moral") is of European origin and has only limited application in the United States. This doctrine reserves a bundle of "paternity rights" to the artist even though the artist may have disposed of his copyright. Among these moral rights is the right to preserve the integrity of the work against alteration, the right to maintain authorship of a work, the right to deny attribution if the author so chooses, and the right to deny exhibition without proper accreditation.

In the United States, an artist has no right to prevent the alteration of his work unless he specifically contracts for that right when he sells his work. A novelist, for instance, would want to include in a contract to sell his book to a movie producer a clause permitting him to veto any adaptation that was not consistent in spirit with the original. Likewise, an artist might wish to insert a similar clause in a contract with a company that proposes to make and market reproductions of one of his paintings. If the artist takes this precaution, he should be protected against the embarrassment that may result if something is published over his name that is unfaithful and damaging to the original. In the absence of such protective language in his contract, the artist may only be able to sue for damages based on injury to his reputation.

The rights best described as "paternity rights" may be guarded by state law in the absence of national copyright law protection. Protection under state law may be realized by applying the theory that it is unfair competition for a person to claim authorship of the work of another or for a person to attribute to an author works of inferior quality. In addition to applying the doctrine of unfair competition, the violation of paternity rights might be resisted as an invasion of privacy, an actionable libel, or a breach of an implied contract. Where an artist feels that he has been injured by the violation of his paternity rights, he is best advised to counsel with an attorney. (Invasion of privacy is discussed on pages 76 to 78 and libel is discussed on pages 78 to 82.)

DROIT DE SUITE, OR THE RIGHT TO ART PROCEEDS

Several European countries—France, Italy, and Germany among others—have enacted an additional provision of their copyright laws known as the *droit de suite*. This right, which has been of recent interest in the United States, entitles an artist or his estate to some portion of the increase in the value of his work upon its resale.

The concept of the *droit de suite* is primarily based upon a belief that the artist does not receive a fair price for his work due to the time lag between its original creation and the subsequent recognition and appreciation of the artist by the public. The plight of the artist, unable to reap the benefits of future sales of his work, is contrasted with the ability of the author to collect royalties as his book rises in popularity. The conclusion drawn by supporters of the *droit de suite* is that the United States copyright laws discriminate unfairly against the artist. To remedy this disparity, it is suggested that for a limited time period, for example the life of the artist plus fifty years, the artist receive a percentage, of say 15 percent, of the appreciated value of his work upon its resale.

Although this proposal appears to be most equitable, it has been criticized on a number of grounds. It is contended that the recent growth in the sale of preliminary drawings enables the artist to cash in on the increase in value of his work. In addition, the proliferation of reproductions may obviate the need for a *droit de suite*. More importantly, however, is the fact that very few artists avail themselves of whatever protection does exist under the copyright laws. Consequently, the actual extent of protection under the present laws cannot be ascertained.

It must also be remembered that the *droit de suite* is totally dependent upon the resale of a work of art. Yet statistics indicate that the likelihood that a given work of art will change hands during the period subject to the *droit de suite* is relatively small. Moreover, the *droit de suite* operates within a rather narrow time span. The right is of no significance if the artist is recognized during his productive period or more than fifty years after his death.

The arguments against a statutory *droit de suite* are somewhat persuasive. Nevertheless, this right is still available to the artist by means of a private contractual arrangement. If the artist chooses to include a provision to this effect in his contract, however, he runs the risk that the collector will purchase other works of art not subject to this restriction. The clause may also result in the unwillingness of a purchaser to pay a high price for a given work. This reduction in price may completely offset the value of the right to the artist. It has also been suggested that the *droit de suite* may be easily evaded by simply disregarding it or by the sale of art in a package, that is, selling a little known work at a high price together with a valuable work and assigning a low price to the work subject to the provision.

The pros and cons of the *droit de suite* can be debated at great length. The purpose of this brief discussion, however, is merely to apprise the artist of the existence of this concept and to point out some of the arguments which militate both in its favor and against it. Whether the artist elects to insert a provision in his contract granting him this right may depend upon a number of factors that will vary according to the circumstances.

INTERNATIONAL COPYRIGHT

In 1954, the United States ratified a major multilateral agreement covering the subject of international copyright. This agreement, known as the Universal Copyright Convention, brought the United States into a partnership which protects works of art copyrighted in member nations. Prior to the Universal Copyright Convention, reciprocal recognition of copyrights depended either on bilateral agreements between individual nations, or upon the covenants of the Berne Convention to which the United States was not a party.

The Universal Copyright Convention, of which the United States is a member, requires a contracting nation to accord works by nationals of other countries party to the convention the same degree of protection as it accords works of its own nationals. Compliance with the formalities of acquiring copyright in the various member states is excused if the notice prescribed by the convention is followed. This notice consists of "©," the year, and the name of the proprietor of the copyright. In essence, therefore, all "foreign" published works covered by the convention are protected automatically in contracting nations by publication with the prescribed notice.

The copyright owner should remember that under the United States Copyright Code, the notice of copyright may include either the word "Copyright," the abbreviation "Copr.," or the symbol "©." The use of the word or abbreviation in place of the symbol does not satisfy the requirements of the Universal Copyright Convention. Therefore, failure to use the legend prescribed by the convention may protect the copyright in the United States, but will not secure reciprocal protection in member nations.

In some instances, nations have become a party to more than one convention. The Buenos Aires Convention, for example, represents the only other attempt the United States has taken toward international copyright protection on a multilateral basis. To date, some eighteen Western Hemisphere countries have ratified the Buenos Aires Convention, which recites that the law of the member country where the work originated determines what formalities must be followed initially to perfect a copyright. The words "Copyright Reserved," "All Rights Reserved," "Derechos Reservados," or the equivalent would most likely meet the requirements of this convention.

In order to gain an effective copyright in a foreign country the provisions of the applicable treaties must be examined. Where a nation is not a party to a multilateral treaty, it may be advisable to have the work of art published in that country so as to become eligible for local copyright protection. It is recommended that a lawyer be consulted before a work of art is published in a foreign country.

CONCLUSION

We have discussed the nature of copyrights, outlined those steps in securing a copyright that can be safely performed by the claimant, and suggested the kinds of problems that might arise which best require the services of a lawyer. It would be wrong to conclude, however, without mentioning once again that the Copyright Office itself is most gracious and helpful in supplying information to those with specific copyright problems. The artist should not hesitate to write the office when he has a copyright problem.

Chapter 3

THE SUBJECT MATTER OF WORKS OF ART

Art is a mode of visual perception and reflects the way the artist sees the world about him. The naive person insists that there is only one way to see the world—the way that it appears to his own immediate vision. This is not true, since we see what we learn to see, and our vision becomes by habit a careful selection of all that there is to see. And what we want to see is determined by our desire to discover or construct a meaningful world. Art in that way becomes a construction of the artist's reality.

In constructing his version of reality, the artist must be concerned with a series of legal wrongs that he may commit in the creative process, or that may be perpetrated upon him in the practice of his profession. The law which permeates the artist's environment, serves to protect an individual from suffering either personal or economic injury. Protection is accorded by permitting recourse to the courts in the following circumstances: (1) where the details of a person's life, his name, his reputation, or a pictorial representation of him are appropriated without obtaining proper consent, there is an *invasion of privacy*; (2) where the property of an individual is unlawfully appropriated for economic gain, it is *unfair competition*; (3) where an untrue statement damages a person's reputation or standing in the community, it is *libel* (written statement) or *slander* (verbal statement); and (4) where an untrue statement damages a product or property, it is *disparagement*. At times, it is difficult to distinguish between wrongs. "John Doe makes a lousy violin," might be interpreted as libel against John Doe, disparagement of his violin, or both.

The artist must also exercise care not to infringe on any rights which, by statute or judicial utterance, are deemed to belong to the public at large. These rights include the integrity of the flag of the United States, the violation of which may be punishable as *desecration*, and the maintenance of contemporary standards of morality, the violation of which may be punishable as *obscenity*. These wrongs and their legal consequences are the subject matter of this chapter.

INVASION OF PRIVACY

The concept that it is a tort, or personal injury, to expose the name, picture, or details of the life of a private citizen is based on the belief that there is an innate right to be left alone—a so-called right of privacy. Invasion of privacy, as an actionable common law tort, came into being in the late 1890's on the theory that, in an increasingly complex society, with a press demanding more and more material for publication, it was necessary to protect a person's right simply to be left alone. Because of its relatively recent development, the law respecting the right of privacy has not developed to the same extent as the law respecting long established torts. Consequently, there is confusion about even quite fundamental issues in this field of the law.

Generally, a person who is not newsworthy has the most compelling argument in favor of protecting a right of privacy. However, even those who have become news-worthy may object to an unsolicited invasion of their private lives when exposure is unrelated to their public image or activities. While it is appropriate to discuss or comment on those aspects of a politician's life that affect his suitability for public office, the details of his family life are generally private, unless he chooses to make them public (as politicians with large and attractive families are wont to do). A person, then, may voluntarily place in the public domain aspects of his life that could not otherwise properly be the subject of comment and criticism.

There are circumstances, however, where the private life of a person is sufficiently interesting to the public that publication without actual or implied consent is permissible. Of course, this statement assumes that the publication is not defamatory or too intimate. A leading case in this area concerned *The New Yorker* magazine profile of a child prodigy who had in his mature years retreated into obscurity. The fact that this person had once been newsworthy and that the public had a reasonable interest in what had happened to him were considered adequate justifications for publishing a report of his present-day circumstance.

The artist is most likely to commit the tort of invasion of privacy by producing and showing a representation of a person without permission. The point has already been made that an artist whose portrait or a photographer whose picture of a subject was rejected might commit an invasion of privacy by showing it or disposing of it to a third person. Obviously, too, a visual work depicting someone who is well known may have increased value. If produced without permission of the subject, such a work may fall into that hazy area where invasion of privacy and unfair competition meet. One way for the artist and photographer to guard against a lawsuit for an invasion of privacy is to ask for written releases from all parties concerned. Care should be exercised when a minor is involved, since releases from minors are void and must be executed by the parent or the guardian. The release should include the purpose to which the released material is to be put. A model release is reproduced in Appendix XIV.

The artist may, of course, be subjected to invasions of his own privacy. He has a right to protect himself from reports of his personal life (though not from comments on his work). Moreover, the artist may resort to a court of law to enjoin others from profiting from the use of his name or his likeness.

The vast majority of cases involving an invasion of privacy occur where there has been a fairly wide publication or distribution of the material constituting the invasion. Mere word of mouth comments (unless uttered on radio or television) probably will not support an action for invasion of privacy, although this issue is still largely unresolved. On the other hand, the amount of publication necessary to support a case for libel or slander has been more thoroughly litigated over the years, and in those cases the most minimal publication will generally support a case.

LIBEL

Any defamatory material that tends to degrade a man in the eyes of his neighbor or to injure his property or business may be considered libelous and give rise to a cause of action for damages suffered. Since libelous material may be published by a writing, an effigy, or a picture, it is therefore advisable for the artist to consider carefully the subject matter of his work before it is published or exhibited.

In most states, no specific injury to the plaintiff needs to be shown in order to collect damages; the injury is presumed from the publication and the character of the statement. The actual damage in a libel case is not harm to the feelings of the person libeled, but the effect on his reputation in society. A person has a right to protect the public image he wishes to display, and it is no defense to a libel charge to argue that most people would not consider the statement defamatory. In a sense, then, libel is the very opposite of invasion of privacy. In an invasion of privacy, the right protected is to have people unaware of one's life; it might be called the right to withdraw, whereas the right to be free from libel is a protection of one's public image.

At times, it is difficult to determine whether certain material will be held libelous. Statements or graphic portrayals may not outwardly appear to libel anyone, or they may accidently libel a person with whom they are not actually concerned. In the first category are statements that do not make direct reference to a specific person, but instead refer to and identify that person by a set of circumstances that would be familiar to some people. In the second category are cases of unintended reference—where, for example, one man is described and something is said of him which, if untrue, would be libelous, and then another man appears who fits this description or who carries the same name. An example of an unintended reference occurred when a newspaper printed a photograph of a man and woman with a caption indicating an intended marriage. In fact, this man was already married. His wife promptly sued the newspaper and received a judgment on the grounds that friends and acquaintances inferred that she was not the wife but, instead, the mistress of the man pictured in the newspaper. In this case, the libellant (newspaper) did not even refer to the plaintiff—the wife—and the statement itself was not libelous, but only damaging when taken in conjunction with the fact, of which the libellant had no knowledge, that the man was already married. In a few states, it is required that where a libel is not clear and complete in itself, the plaintiff has the burden of proving special injury in order to receive a judgment. In these states the inference that there must have been injury is abandoned.

A libel must also be published, which means simply that it must be read by some third party. Therefore, it is not libelous to send an insulting letter to a person, but if the letter is sent by messenger in an unsealed envelope and he reads it, or if it is sent by post card so that post office employees can read it, libel may be found. However, if the recipient permits a private, defamatory letter to be read, the sender is not guilty of publishing. On the other hand, where the sender knows the recipient to be blind or illiterate, so that the letter will have to be read to him, the sender is guilty of publishing a libel.

In a charge of libel, the defendant may respond with the defense that the publication was truthful. However, the burden of proving the truth of the statement is on the defendant. The defendant cannot merely say that he believed the statement true, or that it was told him on good authority, or that the plaintiff has the reputation of doing what was reported. The defendant must actually prove that his statement is essentially true, although some variance in detail is permitted. By placing the burden of proving truthfulness upon the defendant, libel suits become rather difficult to defend. And where the libel charged alleges the commission of a crime, the defendant asserting the truth of his statement may even have to prove it beyond a reasonable doubt; that is, according to the standard of proof that would be used in a criminal court, rather than the civil standard, which is preponderance of the evidence.

Besides asserting that a statement alleged to be libelous is true, a defendant in a libel suit may raise other affirmative defenses. If the plaintiff consents to the libel by publishing the statement himself, or the communication is privileged, the defendant may properly defend his case. Privileged communications include the transmittal of information, damaging or not, where the recipient, an employer or lender for instance, has a legitimate interest in knowing the type of information communicated, or where the sender is attempting to protect his interests or those of one near to him. In the public sphere, one may repeat a statement found in public records and not be guilty of libel, though the statement be false. There will be, of course, a difference of opinion of how public a record must be to qualify in support of this defense.

Another defense to a lawsuit for libel is the right to offer fair comment. For the artist, fair comment is a two-edged sword. The artist may justly comment upon, or even ridicule in words or in graphic art, the works of others. He is, of course, subject to the same sort of comment and criticism from others. Every man who publishes commits himself to the judgment of the public.

It should be evident throughout this discussion that there is no requirement of intent before finding a person guilty of libel. One can libel quite accidentally. Whether a libel is innocent or malicious will be taken into consideration in assessing damages, but not in determining whether a libel has been committed.

DISPARAGEMENT

Disparagement is a form of defamation that reduces or even destroys the value or marketability of property. As in a case of libel, disparagement must be published to a third party, it must be untruthful, and it must refer to the plaintiff. It may, however, be written or spoken and, unlike a libel action, injury is not presumed but must be proven. Just because the artist is unable to sell his work as a result of a disparaging remark, the person who uttered the statement is not necessarily at fault and liability must be demonstrated.

It has been held that a statement charging that a gallery represented a copy to be the original was disparaging where the picture was the original. It has also been held, surprisingly enough, that a publisher had an action for disparagement when it was said of one of its textbooks that it was a laughingstock among intelligent teachers. I use the word "surprisingly" for it would seem that this statement would come within the range of fair comment on literary and artistic matters. And even where it is shown that the artist or author has been unable to sell his products as a result of a disparaging remark that would be called a fair comment, the person who uttered the remark is not liable.

It is also not defamatory to "puff" one's own products, even where there is an implied criticism of another's. A man may generally say, "I produce the best baby-food," or that "oil is safer than gas for heating." If the artist makes a statement to the effect that his work is superior to that of another artist, it may be protected under the recognized privilege to "puff" and also as a fair comment on the work of another. In criticizing the work of another the artist must recognize that there is a fine distinction between fair comment and disparagement.

UNFAIR COMPETITION

Where an artist's work has gained a certain value, it is a form of unfair competition for another party to reap that value without the artist's consent. This legal theory was discussed in the chapter on copyrights, but it is worth repeating that this tort encompasses the wrongful appropriation of an intangible.

Under certain circumstances the prohibition on unfair competition will protect the title of a work of art even though a title is not subject to copyright. This is especially true where a novel has been very successful and a movie producer uses the title to cash in on the reputation of the novel. The title of a painter's work, however, may be subject to wrongful appropriation and exploitation if it is as famous as the *Mona Lisa* or *A Sunday Afternoon on the Island of la Grande Jatte*.

Photographers, in particular, should be aware that

property releases may be required for nonpublic places that are photographed. This problem may arise where a picture is taken of an identifiable building and is later used in an advertisement. If a property release is signed by the owner or agent for the owner, a claim cannot later be made that the use of this photograph constituted unfair competition.

In many respects, the law of unfair competition resembles the law against invasion of privacy. The latter guards against the appropriation of intangibles that are intentionally kept out of the market place. The former protects against the appropriation of those intangibles that are intended to be commercially exploited. In either case, something of value has been taken from the creator.

IMITATION IN ART

Lawsuits for plagiarism are more prevalent in works of fiction, drama, and music than in the graphic arts. Undoubtedly, this paucity of litigation over purported imitation in the graphic arts is a direct result of the artist's understanding that a given period will produce many works of art similar in style and theme. Mature artists understand that art is a combination of personal physical and mental experiences, which are often influenced by the style of other masters. The work of such masters carries an impact that results in waves of influence on younger or less experienced artists. These recognized artists need not necessarily be indignant when they find many of their ideas are used by other artists. Sometimes this is a source of gratification.

In any event, a reticence to press litigation for plagiarism is probably a good thing. It is not desirable that the intellectual and artistic treasures of a society be too stringently restricted by personal monopolies. In a sense, the person who creates a work of art after seeing another, has contributed something of value to society. Frequently, this artist will refine prior techniques or even stimulate greater public enthusiasm for the subject matter. Most likely, this artist's creation will not materially affect the ability of the first artist to dispose of his work, and may even give the work of the first artist greater value and public acceptance.

The right or freedom to imitate does not permit an individual to copy or wrongfully appropriate the creations of another artist. The creator has every right to enjoy the economic fruits of his labors. But, as our copyright law clearly recognizes, the artist should not be entitled to gain a monopoly of a theme, a subject, or an idea.

OBSCENITY

It might seem absurd to many artists, but Michelangelo's famous statue *David* could probably be adjudged obscene by present standards and legally prevented from public display in some cities of the United States. This unusual situation could arise out of a 1973 ruling of the United States Supreme Court rejecting the concept of a "national" standard of morality which, on the whole, has tended to be restrictive in classifying matters as obscene. Now local juries utilizing their own state statutes have the power to determine what is obscene for their communities. But three basic requirements must be met before a work of art can be found obscene. The jury must find that:

(a) the average person, applying contemporary community standards, would find that the work taken as a whole appeals to the prurient interest;

(b) the work depicts or describes, in a patently offensive way, sexual conduct specifically defined by the applicable state law;

(c) the work, taken as a whole, lacks serious literary, artistic, political, or scientific value.

Interestingly, many cities have found that applying a "community standard" at the local level is as difficult as applying a national standard. Who will be able to decide what is the community standard for a rural-college town or a large city with many socioeconomic and ethnic groups? And furthermore, what evidence will a court accept to gauge the moral standards of a community? Also, many states will not be able to apply the Supreme Court ruling because their statutes are either too broad or too vague to be enforced and may be violative of the First and Fourteenth Amendments. The artist should also consider that there are numerous criminal statutes, both state and federal, prohibiting mailing, importation through customs, sale or distribution, exhibition, or possession for sale of obscene materials. It would be wise for an artist to attempt to judge the sensitivities of those who will view his work when he plans its subject matter.

Although not entirely applicable to works of art, the Supreme Court has also held that a motion picture film, which has been judicially determined to be "obscene," can be seized without a hearing but must be preserved as evidence. Upon showing that other copies of the film are not available, the court can permit the seized film to be copied for purposes of exhibition, thereby avoiding a prior restraint or a stopping of the film before a hearing can be held to determine if the showing of the film is illegal.

At present it is not known how this ruling would apply to works of art. But since works of art, unlike film, are unique, a copy could never suffice as a replacement for an original seized from an exhibition.

FLAG DESECRATION

The flag has always been an emotional symbol within our society. Our national anthem reveres it, and the portrait of the marines raising the flag on Iwo Jima has become part of our heritage. Flag and country are often spoken of synonymously; soldiers fight and die for our flag.

Recently alterations and variations of the flag as a means or expression of political protest have become popular. Many statutes, both state and federal, have been enacted to prohibit mutilating, defacing or burning, and other unconventional uses of the flag. Yet, variations of the flag or its design have always been used by many patriotic groups, without interference, even though expressly prohibited by some statutes.

It is generally agreed that many types of flag uses and flag alterations are "symbolic expression" and entitled to constitutional protection as a form of free speech. If, however, there is a valid interest of a state that should be protected, "symbolic expression" can be legally restricted. Two state interests that some courts have employed to restrict variations of the flag are:

(1) to prevent breaches of the peace, such as riots, which might be caused by an unconventional use of the flag;

(2) to prevent desecration of our symbol of national unity.

Art works consisting of a flag hung in effigy, a flag emerging from a toilet bowl, and a flag-covered penis have been ruled to be desecrations by some courts. But some flag desecration statutes are very broad and vague and may infringe on constitutional rights. If, however, an artist wishes to avoid legal problems, he should avoid using flag themes that will offend his viewers.

CONCLUSION

The legal rights and remedies discussed in this chapter by no means exhaust the avenues of protection available to the artist or to those who have suffered injury as a result of the artist's activities. These theories of law should be a starting point, however, for the artist to determine whether he is infringing on the rights of others or whether any of his vested legal rights have been violated. If redress is planned, the artist should seek the advice of a competent attorney.

Chapter 4

THE ARTIST AND TAXES

Hopefully, the artist will receive income from his work. This means that he is likely to have to pay taxes. But, as every citizen, the artist has the right to take advantage of all of the provisions of the Internal Revenue Code that can save him tax money. He must also play by the rules and pay what is due. Several provisions of the Internal Revenue Code are especially relevant to the artist. It is the purpose of this chapter to examine some of these provisions, rather than the income tax structure as a whole. The assumption is that the reader is familiar in a general way with those provisions with which the ordinary taxpayer is likely to come in contact. Our discussion is intended primarily to acquaint the artist with those sections that may apply to him—not a complete income tax guide.

THE TREATMENT OF INCOME

Obviously when an artist sells a painting for cash, he realizes income. But for tax purposes, income is a broad concept that is inclusive of more sources than cash. Income can result when an artist is paid in property, in services, or in cash.

When determining if income has been realized, the Internal Revenue Service looks to see if there has been an accession to wealth. If an artist borrows money, there is no accession since he must repay the money at a later date. But if he loans money, the interest he receives from the borrower would constitute a clear accession to wealth, although the principal repayment of the loan itself would not constitute income. If an artist exchanges one of his own paintings for one produced by another artist, income can result in the amount of the difference between the fair market value of the work received and the cost of producing the work traded.

Sales of paintings produced by the artist and compensation from copyright assignments, commissions, and royalties all produce "ordinary income." Ordinary income results from transactions in an artist's ordinary course of business (producing and selling works of art) and is taxed at ordinary income tax rates. This can be contrasted to capital gains income in which the taxpayer receives favored tax treatment. Capital gains income is taxed at one-half the rate of ordinary income. Generally, capital gains income results from the sale of property held for at least six months for investment purposes rather than from the sale of property held for sale to customers in the ordinary course of business.

Frequently artists purchase works of art from other artists, and where these works are held for over six months from the date of acquisition, these works, upon being sold, are eligible for capital gains treatment. The law considers this property to have been acquired for investment purposes and, thereby, entitled to the 50 percent favored tax treatment.

PRIZES AND AWARDS Artists frequently receive prizes or awards for outstanding accomplishments in their field of interest. With the exception of certain scholarships and fellowships, these will ordinarily be taxable.

Scholarships and fellowship grants are not taxable if the artist is a candidate for a degree at an educational institution or if the award is made by certain nonprofit organizations, including schools and governmental agencies. The exemption for scholarships and fellowship grants covers not only tuition but also amounts given for lodging, incidental travel expense, and equipment. However, if the recipient is required to teach or perform part-time services as a condition to receiving the grant, a portion of the scholarship or fellowship will be considered as compensation for such part-time services and will be taxed.

Apart from such scholarship and fellowship grants, most prizes are taxable as ordinary income. An exception is made, however, for prizes and awards given in recognition of religious, charitable, scientific, education, literary, or civic achievement, provided that the recipient was selected without any action on his part to enter the competition and that he is not required to render substantial future services as a condition to receiving the award. While the recipient cannot apply for the award in the first instance, once he has been selected as a candidate, he will be permitted to fill out necessary forms and to appear for a personal interview without subjecting the award to tax.

If a prize does not fall within any of the exceptions noted above, it will be fully taxable. Where the prize is in some form other than cash, the amount of taxable income is measured by the fair market value of the prize on the day it is received.

AVERAGING INCOME—"SPREADING BACK" A man who earns a steady income of $14,000 per year will pay less income tax in a five-year period than the man who earns $7,500 for four years and $40,000 in the fifth year. Yet both have earned a total of $70,000. This does not seem equitable, especially when the extraordinary income in the fifth year is the final payment on a project that has required five years to complete. It was this inequity that prompted Congress to include an averaging or spreading provision in the Internal Revenue Code. This provision allows the taxpayer to treat some of the extraordinary income as if it had been earned in equal parts over a five-year period.

Assume that in each of four years an artist had $7,500 of taxable income and that in the fifth year he suddenly has $40,000 of taxable income because of two or three large commissions. If he were to pay his taxes the fifth year on the normal basis, his tax would be $14,390 (if he is single and not the head of a household). What happens to the artist's tax if he takes advantage of the income average provision?

First of all, the government does not want to create a complicated tax calculation if there is only a slight variation in income received over a period of years. The income that can be averaged or treated as if it were earned over a five-year period is only that portion of the income which exceeds by more than one-fifth the average income of the preceding four years. It is assumed that a fluctuation of one-fifth or less is not sufficiently abnormal to require income spreading. The amount by which your current year's income exceeds by more than one-fifth your average income for the four prior years is called your "averageable income." In the situation described above, the "averageable income" in the year $40,000 was earned would be $31,000. That is because the actual average income for the four prior years was $7,500 per year; adding one-fifth to that for normal fluctuation brings the four prior years' normal average income to $9,000 per year; the "averageable income" is the amount by which the current year's income ($40,000) exceeds the $9,000 figure, making "averageable income" of $31,000.

If the averageable income turns out to be $3,000 or less, averaging is not permitted, presumably because the tax saving is not worth the trouble; if it exceeds $3,000 you may be eligible to figure your tax by the income averaging method. A special schedule is provided by the Internal Revenue Service for figuring your tax by the income averaging method; at the present time, Schedule G is used for this purpose.

Some artists are not permitted to use income averaging, and others may find that income averaging is not expedient. Among those who cannot use income averaging are persons who are neither citizens nor residents of the United States and persons who, during any of the four prior years, received more than one-half of their support from someone other than their spouse. Income averaging may not be appropriate for those artists who pay taxes at a high rate (over 50 percent) and who may benefit from the 50 percent maximum tax rate on earned taxable income (as opposed to income from dividends, rents, interest, etc.) Further details concerning income averaging can be found in Publication 506, available through the Internal Revenue Service.

DONATING ART TO CHARITY

Most sophisticated art collectors realize that under the tax laws they are entitled to claim a deduction for the

93

fair market value of art that is donated to a recognized charity. By the same token, is the artist who creates art entitled to take a charitable deduction for donating one of his own works to a charitable institution?

Even though the fair market value of a work of art at the date of donation may be substantial, works of art produced by an artist are ordinary income property on which the artist can only deduct the value of his basis (cost of raw materials used in producing the work of art). Consequently, there are no immediate tax benefits available to an artist if he should choose to donate one of his own works to charity. On the other hand, if an artist keeps one of his own works and it is donated to a museum by his estate, the charitable deduction will be based on the market value of his work and not just his costs in creating it.

If an artist purchases a painting by another artist for investment purposes and holds the painting for over six months, it would be capital gains property. If, instead, the painting is held for six months and then donated to a museum which displays the painting, the artist could deduct the fair market value of the painting. This is permitted because the use of the donated property would be related to the exempt function of the museum. But if the museum sold the painting immediately upon receipt and used the proceeds to purchase other paintings or to defray operating expenses, the use of the donated painting would not be related to the exempt function of the recipient. In this case, the artist's deduction would be reduced by 50 percent of the profit that would have been realized had the painting been sold. To illustrate, assume that an artist purchases a painting for $1,000;

three years later he gives it to a museum which immediately resells the work at a time when the painting is worth $4,000. His charitable deduction would be $2,500 ($4,000 fair market value minus one-half of the $3,000 profit that would have been realized had the painting been sold). If, however, the museum exhibits the donated work for a year and then disposes of it, the original use of the painting would probably be related to the exempt function of the museum. Therefore, in order to secure the maximum charitable deduction, it is advisable for the artist to obtain a commitment from the recipient that it will not dispose of the painting for a certain period of time. A more complete explanation of the exempt purposes or function of a charitable organization is set forth on pages 144 to 146 in the discussion of Related Use.

DEDUCTIBILITY OF EXPENSES

An artist seriously engaged in producing art as a livelihood may subtract expenses of producing art from any income received. The mere fact that the artist realizes no profit after expenses are subtracted from receipts does not mean the artist cannot qualify as being in business. However, if art is merely a hobby and the artist only produces an occasional sale, courts have ruled that the expenses of production cannot be deducted in calculating income. Courts reason that in such a case the taxpayer's activities were recreational. If the artist has any doubt on which side of the line he falls, he should consult an attorney.

Assuming that the artist is in business to sell his work, even if it is a side business, there are a number of expenses he can legitimately deduct in calculating his taxable income for the year. In order to report his taxable income, the artist should file Schedule C of Form 1040 with his income tax return. This form may be obtained from the Internal Revenue Service upon request.

In calculating the costs of goods sold on Schedule C, the artist should include the cost of any materials that go into the finished product, the cost of expendable incidentals that do not go directly into the product (for instance, stationery), the wages of hired help (but not wages paid the taxpayer by himself), and other items directly related to producing and selling the product. This last general category would include, for example, the expenses incurred in entertaining prospective purchasers and any expense incurred in traveling to the location where the work is to be exhibited for sale. Travel and entertainment must be for a genuine business purpose and the expenses claimed cannot include those of one's family.

Other business deductions are allowed besides those directly related to the cost of producing a work of art. These include rent or depreciation of business property. The artist will normally have a studio, often in his own residence. If the studio is separate from his residence, the artist may deduct the whole rental cost, as well as the heat, utilities, and the like. Where the artist uses a part of his residence, he may assign to his studio a pro rata share of the costs of running his household. If he uses one of five rooms, he can deduct as a business expense one-fifth of the rent (or depreciation where the building is owned), utilities, heat, etc. If the business use of a specific item or service is greater than one-fifth, a larger share can be deducted; for instance, where the same phone is used for business and pleasure, it may be that, though only one-fifth of the space in the house is used for business, one-half of the phone service is so used. The artist may also discover that if his studio is in his own home, and he moves from one house to another, the Internal Revenue Service will permit him to deduct that portion of his moving expenses that are attributable to his studio.

Where the artist owns property used in his trade or business, and such property has a useful life exceeding one year, he may depreciate this property on one of several scales provided for in the Internal Revenue Code. The choice of methods of depreciation depends upon whether the artist wants to receive the bulk of his deductions as soon as possible, or, whether he prefers to spread them out evenly over a period of years. Probably the biggest problem for the novice record keeper is to determine what is a reasonable life span over which to depreciate a particular article. The Internal Revenue Service produces a pamphlet explaining the concept of depreciation, which includes the appropriate expected useful life of thousands of kinds of articles, from office furniture to buildings, and from heavy machinery to farm animals. If depreciation becomes a problem for the artist, it is best to consult with an accountant or attorney, or an Internal Revenue Service agent.

In order to take advantage of these deductions, the artist must keep records. Keeping detailed and precise ledger accounts is not necessary, though it is likely to simplify the process of calculating income tax. Where keeping a running account of transactions seem excessive, receipts, cancelled checks, bills of sale, can be traced at the end of the year. In all cases, the artist should save any documents which substantiate a deduction should there be a review or audit by the Internal Revenue Service.

SALES TAX

"Sales tax" is a catch-all term that can encompass many diverse revenue raising laws. These taxes are levied by a majority of the states, as well as by many local governments. An artist must consult the laws of his individual state and locality to determine if and in what way he may be affected by a sales tax.

A sales tax, as the name implies, is usually a tax upon sales. In most cases it is assessed by applying a fixed constant tax rate to the value of property or services sold. The state tax rate varies among states, ranging from a low of 2 percent to a high of 7 percent.

In some states an artist selling his works would be required to pay a sales tax, while in other states the liability for payment would be passed on to the purchaser. In the latter case the seller-artist would be required to collect and remit to the state those sales taxes paid by purchasers of his art works. The artist must maintain accurate records reflecting the collection and the payment of these taxes.

If the artist sells his paintings in a state where the seller must pay state sales tax, he can, in most instances, deduct the amount of tax paid from his federal income tax.

INCORPORATION OF THE ARTIST'S BUSINESS

The main attraction to many individuals who incorporate is the chance to save tax dollars. This is especially true in the case of wealthy professionals. These people can set up profit sharing and pension plans by deducting their current income, investing it, and distributing it to themselves at a later date when they might be in a lower tax bracket.

As a general rule, a person organizing a corporation will have to pay a double tax, first on the corporate income and then on the salary and dividends which are distributed after the corporate earnings are taxed. It is possible, under certain conditions, to organize as a "Subchapter S" corporation and pay a single tax as if the income had been earned directly by the individual taxpayer. Taking advantage of a "Subchapter S" status will give the taxpayer the advantages of incorporation (including the opportunity to limit potential liability as discussed on pages 43 to 44) with the exception of some of the fringe benefits noted above.

By incorporation, however, the artist may be incurring legal and accounting expenses for no particular reason. An accountant may have to be hired or the artist may invite federal and state income tax problems. Legal formalities will require the artist to keep current his corporate records and to file certain corporate reports on an annual basis. The corporate form of doing business offers advantages and disadvantages, and each situation should be determined on its own merits.

FOREIGN ARTISTS EARNING INCOME IN THE UNITED STATES

The tax levied on the income of an alien depends on the alien's status as resident or nonresident, and on the

99

LEWIS AND CLARK COLLEGE LIBRARY
PORTLAND, OREGON 97219

nature and source of the alien's income. Once we have sorted out the resident aliens from the nonresident aliens, we can proceed to examine the tax rates applicable to each group. A resident alien is an individual present in the United States who is not a mere transient, and who has no definite intention to terminate his stay. By contrast, an individual who comes to the United States for a particular purpose and can accomplish that purpose promptly, is a transient or a nonresident alien. Under current United States Treasury Regulations, all aliens, because of their alienage, are presumed to be nonresidents unless they have (1) filed a declaration of intention to become a United States citizen under the naturalization laws; (2) filed a Form 1078, certificate of residence; or (3) performed certain acts which reveal a definite intention to acquire residence in the United States.

A resident alien is generally subject to the same income tax liabilities as a United States citizen, including liability for income earned outside the United States; however, to take advantage of the joint return privilege both husband and wife must be residents. If a resident alien pays a tax to a foreign country he is allowed a credit for such taxes on his United States income tax return, if the country of which he is a citizen allows a similar credit to Americans. The reciprocity is required from the country of the alien's citizenship even if this is not the country to which he paid taxes for which he is claiming the credit. If the resident alien cannot claim a credit, he can still take a deduction on his United States income tax return for any foreign taxes paid.

Nonresident aliens are classified according to whether

or not they are engaged in trade or business in the United States. As a rule, if personal services are performed in the United States at any time during the year, this would qualify the individual as one being engaged in trade or business. One so engaged is taxed on income and capital gains derived from sources in the United States at the same rate as United States citizens and is allowed essentially the same deductions with respect to that income. Those not engaged in trade or business in the United States are taxed at a flat 30 percent rate on income not connected with the conduct of trade or business in the United States. Capital gains not connected with the conduct of trade or business in the United States are not taxed unless the nonresident alien is present in the United States for at least 183 days during the taxable year. If the nonresident alien is in the United States for at least 183 days, capital gains not connected with business in the United States are taxed at a flat 30 percent.

UNITED STATES CITIZENS EARNING INCOME ABROAD

The situation may also arise where an artist, who is a citizen of the United States, earns income in a foreign country. An American artist may qualify for preferential tax treatment on income earned in a foreign country by meeting one of two tests: (1) the individual is a bona fide resident of a foreign country, or (2) the individual is physically present in a foreign country for a total of at least 510 full days during any period of 18 consecutive months. The requirement of 510 days (approximately 17 months) in an 18 month consecutive period is flat and unqualified and must be strictly construed. If the artist qualifies under one of these tests, a maximum of $20,000 of foreign income may be excluded from taxable income in any one year. And if the taxpayer has been a bona fide resident of another country (or countries) for an uninterrupted period of 3 years, up to $25,000 may be excluded as long as that bona fide residence outside the United States continues.

The nonresident exemption applies only to earned income; that is, income from wages, commissions, and other forms of compensation for personal services. Royalties are exempt only if the sums received are considered earned income from personal services. An artist who resides in a foreign country may be able to work out an advantageous tax situation by stipulating in his contract that he is to be considered an employee of the royalty user and royalties due him should be in the form of a flat sum, wages, or a commission.

The American artist abroad should also be aware that income tax treaties are in existence between the United States and a number of foreign countries. These treaties are designed to avoid double taxation. Each tax treaty must be examined with care before the artist makes a final decision on its applicability.

PLANNING THE ARTIST'S ESTATE

"Everyone should have a will" is an often heard statement which is, at best, a half-truth. An improperly planned or drawn will can be a greater detriment than no will at all. Because of the complexities involved in estate planning, it is essential that the layman seek professional help. In this discussion, we will consider only a few aspects of estate planning that may be of particular interest to the artist.

A will, subject to certain limitations, allows a person to determine for himself how his property will be distributed upon his death. If an artist dies with a valid will, the executor named in that will takes charge of the estate. It is the duty of the executor to see that taxes are paid and, generally, to conclude the unfinished business left by decedent. After the preliminary matters have been concluded, the executor distributes the residue of the estate according to the terms of the will. The artist should not make the mistake of using friendship as the sole criterion in his choice of an executor. It is advisable to choose an executor who has some legal experience and who possesses knowledge of the commercial aspects of art. This background will better enable the executor to wind up the estate and to maximize the distribution to the heirs.

In the case of a person dying without a valid will (intestate decedent), the individual states have enacted laws governing the distribution of the deceased's property after payment of taxes and expenses. The real estate of an intestate decedent passes according to the laws of the state in which it is located. Personal property (including art works) of an intestate decedent is distributed according to the laws of the state in which the decedent was "domiciled" at the time of death. In most cases a person's domicile will be his home or principal place of residence. All the states provide that the property (real and personal) shall pass in a manner reflecting family ties, and where there is a surviving spouse or children, they take to the exclusion of everyone else. But the states differ as to what proportion of the property should be distributed to which family member. In the case of an intestate decedent without relatives, the estate passes to the state.

The handling of estate taxes is one of the most important considerations involved in estate planning. The federal estate tax is a tax on the amount of property transferred from a decedent's estate, either by the terms of a valid will or by the state laws governing intestate property distribution. This tax is computed on a "taxable" estate after a $60,000 exemption. In most instances there will also be a state inheritance tax which must be paid. An inheritance tax, like an estate tax, in most states is a tax upon the amount of property transferred, but is assessed by the state rather than by the federal government. A credit is allowed in computing the federal estate tax for state inheritance taxes paid.

Federal estate and state inheritance taxes are based upon the fair market value of all property the decedent owned and the value of any interest he held in property at the time of death, or in the case of federal estate tax, at an alternative date within six months after death. Property given away within three years prior to death may also be subject to estate and inheritance taxes. Computing fair market value in cases involving works of art is a very complicated process and frequent source of dispute between taxpayers arriving at low valuations, thereby trying to reduce the estate tax, and Internal Revenue Service computations increasing the valuations and, consequently, increasing the estate taxes. All "relevant" factors and elements which influence that value should be considered. One important case involving the

104

valuation of certain art works held that the prospect of placing a large number of pieces of the same general category on the market at one time is a significant factor which should be considered in determining the fair market value of a deceased artist's art works.

Thoughtful estate planning as reflected in a decedent's will can act to reduce the estate tax burden. Charitable bequests reduce the amount of property on which tax must be paid. Also, an artist's taxable estate will be reduced by the value of that property willed to a surviving spouse, except that this deduction cannot exceed 50 percent of the adjusted gross estate. (Generally the adjusted gross estate is the value of the entire estate minus certain allowable deductions.)

RETIREMENT BENEFITS There are certain provisions of the Internal Revenue Code that make it possible for an artist to plan for a more financially secure retirement. A self-employed artist may contribute up to $2,500 per year or 10 percent of his earned income, whichever is less, to a retirement plan. The value of making a contribution to a retirement plan is that contributions are deductible from gross income in computing adjusted gross income while funds deposited in a retirement plan may build up without being taxed. The tax on the amount contributed, to the extent of the deduction taken, is deferred until such time as the amounts are actually distributed. Benefit payments may not begin before the owner-employee reaches the age of fifty-nine and a half, unless he becomes permanently disabled or dies.

An artist who is self-employed is subject to the self-employment tax in lieu of the social security tax paid by an employee. The purpose of this tax is to provide social security benefits upon reaching the age provided for by law. The amount of self-employment tax due is based upon a certain dollar portion of the net earnings from self-employment and is computed without regard to the number of income tax exemptions to which an individual may be entitled. Thus, self-employment tax may be due even though no income tax is payable. Taxes that are collected during a person's years of gainful employment become the basis upon which benefits are paid both in the event of retirement or disability. The local office of the Department of Health, Education and Welfare should be contacted for more detailed information.

PART II

THE COLLECTOR

Chapter 5

PURCHASING ART

In purchasing a work of art, the collector pays for at least three different things—the quality of the work, the reputation of the artist, and the certainty that the named artist actually created the work. The prominent collector, Richard Rush, urges in his book *Art As an Investment* that the buyer look first for quality. That is sound advice; if the artist loses favor, as have many English landscape and portrait painters for instance, or if it is later proven that the painting had been wrongly attributed to a master when it was the work of a student, what is left but the painting? If it can be treasured for itself, the money spent for the work is not all lost.

If we limited ourselves to *nouveau riche* buying for investment, our audience would be limited indeed—not only because those people are relatively few in number, but also because most have attorneys on retainer. The collector buying modestly is probably investing his money in the safest manner. He may be purchasing the works of contemporaries, or of the lesser lights of earlier times. In either event, he is likely to avoid one of the two pitfalls awaiting the unwary collector of expensive works—false attribution. And if the work purchased is pleasing, the modest buyer need not be seriously disturbed by market fluctuations. If prices fall, and they cannot fall too far, the opportunity to enjoy the work is likely to be worth the price, and if they rise, the collector has a windfall.

It is the collector investing thousands of dollars in a single piece of art who must take extreme precautions to insure authenticity, for it is the big names whose works are forged, or purposely copied. The collector who is ready to acquire the work of a great master must never forget the name of Hans van Meegeren, an obscure Dutch artist who, during the days preceding the Second World War, forged and sold paintings that were accepted by well-known critics as genuine Vermeers. The discovery that these were forgeries shocked the art world, for several had been purchased for hundreds of thousands of dollars by museums and prominent collectors. These works are now worth only a few hundred dollars, mainly as curiosities. From a legal point of view, it was debatable whether the crime of forgery had been committed by van Meegeren, since he did not imitate anything, but only painted in Vermeer's style and manner.

But forgery is by no means the only source of confusion respecting the attribution and authenticity of old paintings. Copying was once the standard method by which artists taught their apprentices, and to execute a good copy in the days before mechanical reproduction was considered thoroughly respectable. Today, in Europe there are virtual painting factories turning out copies of paintings in the style of well-known artists.

These copyists are not necessarily dishonest. But despite their best intentions, the attribution given a painting once it is out of their possession is out of their control. The result is that there are doubtless tens of thousands of originally honest copies and probably thousands of intentional forgeries, created by more or less apt pupils, floating around to confuse the critic, the dealer, and the purchaser.

IS THE WORK GENUINE?

PAINTINGS The real concern of the purchaser of a painting is to acquire an authentic work created by the artist to whom it is attributed. Distinguishing between an authentic painting and a fake, however, is not always an easy task.

The legal definition of "forgery" is basically a narrow one, as a forgery must be of a document or writing. However, in connection with paintings and pictorial art generally, "forgery" is normally used in its popular rather than legal connotation. In artistic parlance, forgeries or fakes may be created by (1) painting in the style of a recognized artist, but not copying an existing picture; (2) forging a specific original solely for the purpose of representing it as the original itself; (3) combining fragments from paintings by a specific artist into new compositions which are then attributed to that artist; (4) attributing a painting from the school of a recognized artist to the master by forging his signature; and (5) ascribing a group of paintings to a nonexistent artist.

Several precautionary measures may be taken by the

purchaser of a suspected fake. If the artist is alive, the first and preferred method is to ask the artist if the work is authentic. In some cases, however, artists deliberately disavow earlier works with which they later became disenchanted.

Sometimes the back of a picture will have customs stamps and other marks of pedigree, including who has owned it and where it has been exhibited. If this information is not available and the work seems worthy of further investigation because of apparent age and quality, a chemical analysis of the pigments can be undertaken. Such an analysis can reveal the age of the pigments and, in some cases, it is known whether or not a given pigment was available to or used by a given artist. Ultraviolet light can show whether or not a painting has been retouched. An expert can guess from the very brush strokes whether or not a work is genuine. This kind of research costs money; it is performed by the more reputable galleries, and it is for this reason that paintings cost more at these galleries. In effect, the purchaser is paying for certain attribution and warranties these galleries provide.

The person who is knowledgeable in a certain school of art and who buys for quality may well prefer to trust his own judgment on the value of the work; such a person can save money at smaller galleries and auction houses where there may be no facilities for authentication. But it is wise, whenever a substantial sum of money is involved, to have a work authenticated by one qualified to do so. A museum official or the art department of a local college may well be able to help. These institutions are often glad to do so, at least partly in the hope that someday the collector will donate works to them. (See Appendix XV for an Application for Expert Opinion as to Authenticity.)

Many reputable art dealers have long had a policy of insuring the genuineness of their merchandise, but many others follow the ancient rule of "caveat emptor" —let the buyer beware. Where the dealer refuses to take back a work of questionable authenticity, there are several options available to the collector. In New York, a statute was enacted in 1966 which provides that a dealer who sells a painting as a work of a particular artist must give a refund to his customer if the buyer can establish that the painting was not that artist's work. As a result of this protective legislation, the purchaser is no longer in the position where he is uncertain whether or not the written description set forth in the bill of sale is sufficient to constitute a warranty that the work is genuine. A warranty is now automatic if the full name of the artist is written on the bill of sale.

A collector who has been victimized and looks to the criminal law for assistance will find that there are a number of problems which may arise in the prosecution of art fraud cases under existing criminal statutes. If a would-be forger is accused of larceny under false pretenses, the prosecutor must establish not only that the seller said that he was offering an authentic "Renoir," but that he knew the work was not, in fact, a "Renoir." In some states there is a statute relating to counterfeiting a trademark. Since the artist's signature is a trademark, a forgery of the signature is a violation of the law. However, such a violation is often difficult to prove since the prosecutor must establish that the seller actually did the counterfeiting.

The Uniform Commercial Code has been adopted by most states and can offer some protection for the purchaser of a fake. But the buyer's success in an action against the seller will depend greatly upon what the seller has warranted. The Uniform Commercial Code states that an express warranty arises when a seller makes a promise or affirmation of fact relating to the work of art which is the heart of the bargain. In truth, however, only the artist himself can authenticate, for certain, his own work. Hence any statement, affirmation of fact, or promise made by the seller to the buyer, with respect to authentication by anyone other than the artist himself could be interpreted as merely the seller's opinion or "sales talk." Realistically, what is or is not an opinion or sales talk is more a question of degree to be determined by a jury weighing all the facts and circumstances. When a seller makes a statement that the buyer reasonably interprets as being essential and more than mere opinion or sales talk, then an express warranty has been made. If a work of art proves not to be what the seller has expressly warranted, the transaction can be rescinded.

The best possible indication that a seller has made an express warranty can be found in the sales price paid. The fact that a seller stated that a painting was by "Renoir" could be merely his opinion. If the seller also stated that the value of that painting was that of a "Renoir," it could be interpreted as sales talk. But when these statements occur together, and there is a sale at that stated value, there is a strong presumption that an express warranty of genuineness has been made by the seller that the painting is, in fact, a "Renoir." Most courts will presume that a buyer would not pay a substantial price for anything less than a binding obligation on the part of the seller to transfer ownership to an authentic work by "Renoir."

PRINTS Prints are often reproduced or faked and sold to unknowing purchasers as originals. Here the collector's problem is to differentiate between an "original" print and a reproduction. A print is generally made by using one of the following techniques: (a) stencil process (applying coloring or ink to perforated parts of a master sheet, e.g., silk screen); (b) lithography (printing from an image on stone); (c) intaglio, e.g., etchings or engravings; and (d) relief, e.g., woodcuts.

The Print Council of America, a nonprofit organization fostering the creation and appreciation of fine prints, has outlined three requirements for an "original" print: (a) the artist alone has created the master image in or upon the plate, stone, wood block, or other material for the purpose of creating the print; (b) the print is made by the artist or pursuant to his directions; and (c) the finished print is approved by the artist.

A print's value is judged by the degree of active participation by the artist himself; hence, to the extent that the artist permits the work to be performed by others, the value is reduced. Value also depends on the number of the impression, the condition of the print, the number of editions, and the size of the edition.

Reproductions, by contrast, are generally made by

photomechanical and other processes, independent of the artist's supervision and without his final approval. Because of the artistry involved, there is a difference in value between an "original" print and a reproduction. This disparity has attracted irresponsible art dealers who sometimes represent an unlimited edition as being limited, peddle photographic reproductions of original prints, or add the artist's signature (genuine or false) after the print has been published. Obviously, the purchaser does not want to pay a premium for an "original" print only to discover that he has acquired a reproduction. A buyer is advised to ask the seller to state on the invoice that the print he has purchased is an "original." Any hesitation on the part of the dealer should warn the purchaser that he may not be buying an "original."

In Illinois and California the buyer need not rely solely on the integrity of the dealer. These states have enacted so-called "Print Bills" which provide that no print shall be intentionally sold, at wholesale or retail, unless a written invoice or receipt for the purchase price or a certificate given to the buyer clearly discloses all of the basic details of the print. If the dealer describes the print as a "reproduction," he need not furnish any of the informational details, unless he claims that the print was published in a signed, numbered, or limited edition. Under the "Print Bills," each buyer should be furnished with these informational details; (a) the name of the artist and the year when printed; (b) whether the print is an etching, engraving, woodcut, lithograph, or whether the seller does not know; (c) whether the edition is being offered as a limited edition, and, if so, the total size of the edition; (d) whether the plate from which the print was run has been destroyed, effaced, altered, defaced, or canceled after the current edition, or whether the seller does not know; (e) if there were any prior editions from the same plate, the series number of the current edition, and the total size of all prior editions; (f) whether the edition is a posthumous edition or restrike, and, if so, whether the plate has been reworked; and (g) the name of the workshop, if any, which printed the edition. Since this law specifies those facts which the seller must make known to the buyer, a seller cannot later claim that he did not expressly represent or warrant the quality and characteristic of the print.

In the absence of an intention to deceive, a person who offers or sells a print in violation of the law shall return to the buyer, upon tender of the print, the purchase price plus interest at the legal rate. Where a person knowingly misrepresents the print, the purchaser is entitled to recover three times the purchase price. If a print sells for less than a certain amount, it may not be covered by the law. For example, in Illinois the minimum purchase price is $50.00 ($60.00 if framed) and in California, $25.00 ($40.00 if framed).

SCULPTURE The purchase of sculpture presents problems not associated with the acquisition of a painting. A sculptured work may be created by one of three basic techniques: (1) fashioning an object out of a material which hardens, e.g., clay, plaster, or cement; (2) carving an object from a hard material, e.g., stone or wood; and (3) modeling a prototype and making a replica by casting.

Authentication problems generally arise when the sculpture is produced from a prototype since it is difficult to assess the number of casts made. Unfortunately, even the artist's assurance that the cast was made by him or under his supervision is not always reliable. Modern techniques often prevent the most conscientious sculptor from controlling the production of casts in excess of an authorized edition. "If you can make one, you can make a thousand," said one expert, who noted that a bronze can be reproduced to within one one-thousandth of an inch accuracy. Even when the edition is carefully controlled, the artist's failure to sign and number his work may cause confusion.

PHOTOGRAPHS Until recently, photographs, although often admired, have seldom been seriously collected. In fact, the proposition that photography deserves serious critical study has been simply unintelligible to leaders of some art museums. As a result, knowledge and opinions of experts concerning the legal problems inherent in collecting photographs are being continually refined.

It appears that most of the same problems associated with buying prints apply to purchasing photographs. Some knowledgeable collectors of photographs even draw an analogy between lithography and photography since the stone used in making a lithograph is similar in many respects to the negative used in making a photograph.

At the present time there are no published requirements for "originality" of photographs as in the case of prints. Indeed, the prospective buyer must fend for

116

himself in differentiating between a so-called "original" and a restrike or a copy. One question that is often asked is whether the particular photographer processes his own prints or whether he hires a skilled printmaker. If the photographer customarily makes his own prints and one of his prints happens to be produced by a print-maker, is the print made by the printmaker considered an "original"? Originality also requires an investigation of whether the work is a vintage print or simply a product of a later period, as frequently occurs in the case of a restrike. Since most photographers do not take the precaution of signing and numbering their prints, careful research of the photographer's techniques and the manner and methods of printing becomes essential to the collector.

Unfortunately photography is still in an embryonic stage with respect to questions of originality and authenticity. Therefore, it is suggested that the uninformed buyer seek expert advice before investing in a photograph.

AUCTIONS

One of the most common ways to buy and sell art is the public auction. This has long been true. Christie's auction house in London, still going strong, was in business at the time of the American Revolution. Today, the art auction is probably more popular than it has ever been. Since the end of the Second World War, prices for works of art, with some notable exceptions, have risen so rapidly that sales prices at larger auctions are often front page news.

The auction, at least theoretically, provides a means

117

of accurately determining current market values. The "theoretically" must be added, for auctions are subject to manipulation and to waves of emotion. Bidding may be dampened by casting aspersions on authenticity or by art dealers who agree that only one of them will bid for a specific picture. If the one dealer is successful, the picture is then auctioned privately among the participating dealers, and they share the profit made at the second sale. If dealers have a surplus of works by a certain artist, they may bid up the price of a painting being sold at auction to give the impression that the particular artist is gaining in popularity. Waves of enthusiasm among collectors may also raise auction prices well above the level experts would consider reasonable. Still, as a general rule, auction prices are lower than those quoted at important galleries.

The owner of an art work may bid for his own property in the hopes of raising the price. This practice, where it is not made clear that the owner is bidding, is fraudulent. A purchaser may rescind a sale if it is later discovered that the owner or his agents were bidding to force up the price.

LEGAL MECHANICS OF AN AUCTION In law, an auction is simply a sale with a special method for determining price. There are special rules for auctions related to the bidding mechanism for setting price, but otherwise, auctions are governed by the general laws concerning sales. Unlike statutory copyright legislation, which is national, the law of sales and auctions is local in character. Each state has its own sales and auction laws; there is, however, a general similarity among the states and many have adopted uniform acts drafted by panels of experts.

When an auctioneer puts a work of art up for sale, he is not making an offer to sell it to the highest bidder; it is the bidder who makes the offer. The auctioneer says in effect, "How much am I offered?" And, if he does not hear an offer he considers adequate, he may decline all those that are made. When a person responds with a bid that is recognized by the auctioneer, each prior bid is discharged. The last recognized bid is the only outstanding offer; the auctioneer indicates acceptance of the outstanding offer, or bid, by dropping his gavel. Any bidder (offeror) may, by giving notice to the auctioneer, withdraw his bid (offer) before the fall of the gavel. Once the gavel is banged, however, the bidder cannot change his mind; his offer has been accepted and a binding contract has been entered.

The auctioneer's corresponding right to withdraw a property from the sale exists unless the auction is described as "without reserve," or it is otherwise indicated that the goods will be sold to the highest bidder. The right to withdraw property from sale has been used to justify denying a person damages when, after traveling from Africa to New York to attend an auction, the auction was cancelled. The announcement of an auction, then, is no guarantee to a prospective bidder that an auction will take place. However, the terms of sale and other rules pertaining to the auction that have been advertised must be followed, unless notice is given to the contrary.

Where a sale is without reserve, no lot may be withdrawn after even one bid has been made on it regardless of the auctioneer's feeling that the bid price is too low. Lots may be withdrawn, however, before the bidding has begun; consequently, the traveler, frustrated by having the auction cancelled, has no more protection when the auction is without reserve.

The reserve is usually a minimum price below which the auctioneer is not empowered to sell. Sometimes the reserve price may be advertised, although, in practice, the upset price is generally kept secret. Auctioneers prefer not to disclose the minimum price since too low a reserve may dampen the market. The reserve right may also be in the form of permission to the auctioneer to use his discretion in rejecting bids.

In the absence of special conditions of sale, title to the auctioned property passes when the gavel is knocked down and the auctioneer accepts the bid. With the passage of title to the buyer the risk of loss also passes. This means that the buyer bears any subsequent loss by fire or theft, unless otherwise specified by the terms of the auction.

WARRANTIES AT AUCTIONS The big auction houses, and undoubtedly reputable smaller ones as well, make no warranty of the catalogue description, authenticity, or condition of any paintings offered at auction. Their catalogues will usually set forth the terms and conditions of sale (see Appendix XVI). Purchasers are normally given the opportunity to examine the works before the auction so that they can determine whether the property is suitable for purchase. There is, however, a code commonly used in catalogue descriptions to indicate the gallery's position concerning attribution: the artist's full name indicates the greatest certainty; last name plus first initial lesser certainty; and the last name alone indicates a serious doubt of authenticity.

When an auctioneer does make a warranty, he or his employer is bound by it. If such warranties are given informally, they are nevertheless enforceable. This is especially true where the auctioneer is or purports to be knowledgeable and well informed, and it is clear that the bidder is not an expert and is relying on the auctioneer's judgment. A catalogue description may also be taken as a warranty where there is no disclaimer. The fact that there have been very few cases in American courts concerning auction warranties on art or antiques suggests that art auctioneers are pretty careful about making claims.

One recent case has significant overtones with respect to the strength of an auctioneer's disclaimers. In this case, buyers who unknowingly purchased fake paintings at an auction conducted by a reputable auction house, sued the house to recover the purchase price they paid. The court ruled that the purchasers were not entitled to recover their money in view of the fact that the auction catalogue was clearly designed to disclaim any warranty or representation of genuineness. Moreover, the court reasoned that the competitive pricing of the bids reflected the degree of certainty with which these paintings could be authenticated and established as the works of the ascribed artist. At the time this auction occurred neither statutory nor case law recognized that the expressed opinion or judgment of the seller could give rise to any implied warranty of authenticity. Given the same set of facts occurring today, a court might well reach a contrary decision.

The one thing the auctioneer or his principal clearly warrants is that he has good title to the picture he is selling. This means that no one can come to the buyer at a later date and claim that this piece is really his and the auctioneer had no business selling it. Where there is a defect in title and the auctioneer has revealed the name of the seller to the successful bidder prior to the auction, the purchaser's complaint should be directed to the actual seller. The point is that when the buyer knows the identity of the seller, he is, in effect, relying on the seller to deliver clear title. But where the true seller is not indentified, the auctioneer is liable for any failure to pass good title. The auctioneer may also be liable to the buyer if other warranties have been given, although the legal test may be whether the warranty was made within the scope of authority given the auctioneer by the seller. This problem will not affect the right of the buyer to sue for damages or for rescission of the purchase; rather it will only determine who the buyer is able to sue. Where there is any doubt concerning the proper party to sue, it is best for the buyer to join both the seller and the auctioneer as joint defendants.

SPECIFIC PERFORMANCE AS A REMEDY FOR FAILURE TO DELIVER The Anglo-American law has traditionally been divided into two broad categories—law and equity. Equity developed in England in early modern times to provide remedies in situations where the traditional law courts were unable to assist. Law may have been unable to help because it gave no remedy at all, or because it gave an inadequate one. Basically, the only civil remedy at law was the payment of money. On the other hand, equity courts had the power to order people to do things other than to pay money. One equitable remedy is to order people to perform a contract, whereas a court of law could require only the payment of money damages when a contract was not performed.

Traditionally, courts of equity will not order the performance of a contract unless the subject matter of the contract is unique. Therefore, a plaintiff cannot seek an equitable remedy when a painter who had agreed to paint his house refuses to do so. This plaintiff can only go to a court of law to ask for money damages, which is usually the difference between the price settled on in the contested contract and the price the plaintiff had to pay to find someone else to do the job. However, a plaintiff can file an action in equity to request specific performance when a gallery owner who agreed to sell a Rembrandt later changes his mind and refuses to deliver the painting. In this case, a court of equity will act because it is assumed that no money damages will be sufficient to purchase an equivalent to the Rembrandt painting, because there is no substitute for that particular painting. Most, if not all, contracts for the purchase of fine art works are specifically enforceable.

As a general matter there is no longer a distinction between a court of equity and a court of law. However, the traditional equitable remedies are still available only in those circumstances in which the old equity courts would act. The remedy of specific performance, a traditional equitable remedy, would be available in appropriate circumstances regardless of whether the purchase was made at an auction, a gallery, or from a private individual.

DUTY OF AUCTIONEER TO SELLER The occasion may arise when a collector decides to dispose of some or all of his works by means of an auction. The auctioneer is the owner's agent, subject to the same general rules of agency as is the gallery that sells an artist's works on a commission basis (see pages 35 to 40). There is no problem, however, respecting giving public notice that the agency relationship of an auctioneer is terminated. It is generally recognized that such an agency terminates with the conclusion of the auction.

The auctioneer has the same duty to the owner as the gallery to the artist—to care for the works put in his possession. Both are, as holders of the works, bailees for hire. The bailee for hire (a person paid to hold or handle the goods of another) is bound to exercise what is called ordinary care—the care a person would take of his own property. This rule applies where there is no specific contract detailing the degree of liability assumed by the bailee. A gallery or auction house will prefer, of course, to reduce its own liability as bailee, either by contracting out or by making arrangements for insurance. In dealing with a bailee, an artist or owner should want to clarify the degree of the bailee's liability, and is strongly urged to arrange for either himself or the bailee to purchase adequate insurance coverage.

PURCHASE FROM A GALLERY
OR PRIVATE PERSON

In an auction, price is set by bidding; the terms of sale and applicable warranties are usually settled by the rules for the auction circulated by the auctioneer. In a direct sale, price, warranties, and terms of purchase are proper subjects of negotiation, though some galleries may set their terms and leave it to the purchaser simply to accept or reject them. No rules can be given for effective bargaining, other than that the purchaser should keep in mind that he has certain matters to settle when he does make a direct purchase.

As suggested earlier, price may be contingent on certain other aspects of the deal. For example, a preferential price may be given for cash. Then, too, the price is likely to be higher when dealing with experts willing and able to authenticate a work.

In the majority of cases, well-known galleries have sufficient knowledge or sufficient concern with their reputation to be willing to guarantee a work; where that is not true, at least a guaranteed history of ownership may be available. And some galleries, in lieu of, or in addition to other guarantees, will enter into buy-back agreements. Buy-back contracts can be written so as to require the gallery to repay the purchase price or to credit the purchase price or value toward another work whenever the purchaser should want to return the picture; they may also limit the responsibility to buy-back to certain situations, such as when doubt is cast upon authenticity. The terms of the buy-back agreement are also subject to negotiation. In dealing with the established gallery, one is reasonably certain to find one or another of these procedures adopted as a standard method of operation. As long as the adopted method provides reasonable protection, there is probably little point in bargaining for a variation.

Lesser galleries usually sell art more cheaply; they are more interested in rapid turnover and they usually lack facilities for authenticating. They are less likely to be willing to guarantee authenticity. Many reasonable and sometimes very excellent buys may be found in such galleries, but the buyer must be willing to rely upon his own taste and artistic erudition in making a selection.

Despite the fact that the reputable lesser gallery may be reluctant, or unable, to give guarantees on the authenticity of any but contemporary works, warranties may, in some instances, arise more or less unintentionally. Warranties that might otherwise come into being respecting possible defects or conditions that could be detected by a surface examination are waived when the purchaser examines the item or refuses to do so despite a specific request of the seller. Warranties against hidden defects are not waived by the buyer's examination. The reasons behind these rules should be obvious.

In the event that a work of art is warranted or represented to a buyer to be an original or a print, but later turns out to be a copy or a reproduction, what should be the proper measure of damages? This becomes an interesting question if the value of the work of art, assuming it had been authentic in the first instance, has increased since the date of purchase. Where there is not a controlling statute that sets the measurement of damages, some courts have held that the buyer is only entitled to a refund of the purchase price plus interest. However, this judicial reasoning overlooks the fact that the injured buyer will not be adequately compensated if he only receives his money back. Thus, by limiting recovery to one's initial investment, a court would be denying that the buyer has really suffered any damage.

An aggrieved buyer would be better advised to sue for the present value of the work of art, assuming it to be genuine. This theory of damages would reflect what the buyer had actually lost. At the same time it would award the buyer that loss which directly and naturally resulted from the seller's breach of warranty and would place him in as good a position as he would have occupied if the contract had been honored. If a court accepts this theory of damages, the buyer will still have to present evidence of the value of the work of art.

RENTAL ARRANGEMENTS

Two types of rental arrangements are widely used. The first is a straight rental agreement where the borrower is expected to return the piece at the end of the rental period. The second is a rental-purchase plan, whereby the rental fee may be applied to the purchase price. The first type is used by institutions with permanent circulating collections; the second is used primarily by galleries or rental outlets in museums whose main concern is selling to the public.

The rental-purchase plan is particularly attractive to buyers who are looking for works of art that they can enjoy. This plan permits the borrower to live with an object for a period of time before making a final commitment to purchase. This arrangement serves much the same function as the buy-back, but is probably more advantageous for the gallery or rental outlet that accepts works of art on consignment.

The rental agreement itself is usually a very simple document (see Appendix XVII). The borrower agrees to use the picture for display in his own home only, to respect the common law copyright (see pages 64 to 65), and to be liable for damage or deterioration resulting from his gross negligence. Insurance against other risks will usually be provided; the borrower should make sure, however, that he understands just what protection is specified in the agreement.

The rental-purchase plan provides, in addition, that the rent paid may be applied toward the purchase price. A two-month period seems to be a commonly accepted rental period, although one or more renewals may be permitted. A Chicago gallery, for instance, using the rental-purchase plan allows a two-month rental and a two-month renewal, the rent for both periods being applicable to the purchase price.

PURCHASING FROM THE ARTIST

With the spread of art fairs, another phenomenon of the postwar art boom, more and more individuals have easy and direct access to practicing artists interested in selling their works. Artists displaying at fairs range from rank amateurs to those having achieved substantial local recognition. The well-established artist, however, is less likely to exhibit for several reasons. First, he may have an exclusive sales arrangement with a gallery; second, he may be executing more ambitious works for which he would have to charge more than the typical art fair patron is prepared to spend; or third, he may simply find an art fair more exhausting and time consuming than it is worth. The mere fact that a recognized artist is less likely to display his work at an art fair should not discourage a collector from buying at a fair. In fact, works of good quality can often be obtained quite reasonably, and there is no middleman or dealer to be compensated. There is, of course, no problem with attribution; the only question is the quality and price of the work. Since a sale is often consummated on the spot, there is little likelihood that problems pertaining to delivery of the piece will arise, unless an arrangement is made to pay for and pick up a work at a later time. About the only type of warranty that might be inferred in this type of a transaction is that the work is done in such manner that it will not immediately fade or disintegrate.

What is true for a purchase at an art fair is true for any direct purchase from an artist. Complications are likely to arise only where works are commissioned or where the artist has an exclusive sales arrangement with a dealer or gallery. If the latter situation arises, a person who purchases from the artist without knowledge of the agency relationship will have no responsibility to reimburse the agent for a commission. It is the artist who will have breached his contract and most probably be subject to a lawsuit for damages. On the other hand, if the purchaser is aware of the artist's contract with a dealer, the purchaser may be subjected to a claim for commissions by the dealer. The prudent buyer should inquire if the artist has such a relationship, but it is not clear just how exhaustive this inquiry must be to claim that a purchase was consummated without knowledge.

FRAMING WORKS OF ART

Understandably, the framing of a work of art is very vital, for upon it will depend much of its preservation.

Anyone sending a valuable painting to be framed must be certain that there is adequate insurance to cover shipment to and from the framer. Most framers will disclaim all liability for, or responsibility to insure against, any loss or damage occurring while the painting is in the hands of an independent carrier.

When an art work is received by the framer, a bailment is created. A party entering into a bailment should seek counsel because the law allows almost total freedom of the parties involved to determine conditions of liability. (See page 124.) The framer will usually be well counseled and armed with printed forms designed to limit his liability to a minimum. (See Appendix XVIII.)

In the absence of any agreement to the contrary, a framer (bailee) will generally only be liable for loss or damage to art works which result from his own negligence. The framer will not be liable for accidental loss or damage that is not negligent and will not be under a legal duty to insure against such loss or damage. The owner of the painting, therefore, must also be certain to insure against nonnegligent loss while the piece is in the possession of the framer.

SYNDICATIONS

With the prices of great masterpieces rising to phenomenal levels, it is not uncommon for groups of art

130

dealers or private investors to purchase these art objects, either for immediate resale or to hold as a long-term speculation. Generally, these groups form a syndicate or partnership and each member holds an undivided interest in the property proportional to his respective investment. It may be assumed that persons who enter such agreements are sophisticated art investors and do so with appropriate legal advice.

In a syndicate purchase, the participant is generally approached by a promoter to invest a certain sum of money in return for an undivided interest in the work of art. Where the promoter approaches a great number of prospective investors, there may be some question as to whether the undivided interest is a "security," subject to the provisions of the Securities Act of 1933, as amended, and various state laws. The chief purposes of these laws are to obtain full, fair, and accurate disclosure of the character of securities offered for sale and to prevent fraud in the sale of securities. If a person is contacted by an art syndicate promoter, he is best advised to check out the deal thoroughly and to consult an attorney before committing himself.

COMPANIES INVESTING IN ART

The recent phenomena of soaring art prices has offered promoters an opportunity to organize companies to buy and sell art works. Investors, knowing little or nothing about collecting art itself, have become eager buyers for shares of these companies. Some promoters have even confessed in their prospectuses that they have had limited experience with the type of business in which they plan to engage.

For the most part, these art companies found the

131

high-class art auction market too risky for their initial investments. Instead, they sought out relatively unknown artists who would agree to work and produce for them. These companies then proceeded to create their own market for their artists' work by opening galleries and franchising others to sell "original oil paintings" and "blue chip art works" to the public.

Despite initial favorable public reaction to shares in these companies, these investments have been unrewarding. Lack of adequate financing and an inability to make a profit have been the primary causes of failure. Then, too, respected art critics, museums, and dealer associations have been reluctant to endorse the concept of mass marketing of art. Investors should exercise great caution in buying shares of these art companies.

Chapter 6

TAX PROBLEMS OF COLLECTORS
AND
DEALERS

Art collectors and art dealers must pay taxes on income derived from the sale of art, but the collector and the dealer who purchase art work as an investment and not for sale in the ordinary course of business may both be eligible to receive preferential income tax treatment on any profit. In the hands of a collector or a dealer-investor, a work of art may be a capital asset, the sale of which will be taxed at the capital gains rate. Normally, however, a dealer who sells works of art from inventory must report any profits as taxable income. There may also be tax questions on the feasibility of contributing art works to a charitable institution. For the most part, this chapter will be concerned with the tax consequences of a sale or a contribution of art works.

GAINS ON THE SALE OF ART

For the individual (noncorporate) taxpayer two alternative preferences are given for income classifiable as long-term capital gains—gains from the sale of assets held for more than six months. The tax is on *net* long-term capital gains. The problem of what is net arises only when a taxpayer also has losses from the sale of short- or long-term capital assets. Assuming no losses to complicate the situation, the taxpayer may either deduct from his gross income 50 percent of his capital gains, so that, in effect, he pays the normal tax rate on only one-half his gains, or he may elect to pay a 25 percent tax on capital gains of up to $50,000 and at a regular rate for any excess. The first alternative is to be preferred for a person in a lower tax bracket, while the second benefits one in a higher tax bracket. The alternative which results in the greatest saving can be determined by calculating the tax by both methods and comparing the results. The capital gains provisions are, therefore, not exclusively for the advantage of millionaires. Any person selling a capital asset may conserve tax dollars; it is just that the millionaire saves more.

The favorable treatment given the sale of capital assets is justified by more or less reasonable arguments—that it would be unfair to tax fully the income from the sale of an asset held for several years when the income is all realized in one year, and that high taxes on the transfer of assets will discourage the mobility of capital —and by popular feelings that have little or no relation to economic reality—that nonrecurring income is somehow not income at all. But, when you come right down to it, neither economic nor accounting analyses provide any basis for the distinction. The boundary line between capital gain and ordinary income has been drawn by considering different types of transactions and granting or denying the favorable treatment for policy reasons or merely because of political pressures.

The result is a law that gives capital gains treatment to gain from sales of what are classed as "capital assets." The problem of deciding what is and what is not to be accorded special treatment is determined by the definition of capital assets. Capital assets are defined by the Internal Revenue Code as all property with certain important exceptions. One exception is property held for sale to customers in the ordinary course of the taxpayer's trade or business. A collector who, outside of his normal course of business, buys a painting and holds it for the requisite period (at least six consecutive months) may report the profit from a sale as a capital gain. The dealer, however, because his business is to sell art works, will have a difficult time proving that a work was not held for sale in his ordinary course of business. In the case of a dealer attempting to claim capital gains treatment on the sale of art works, the Internal Revenue Service will scrutinize the transaction for "factors which would place the sale in the dealer's normal course of business." The dealer must show that the sale was "extraordinary" and not in his normal course of business to receive capital gains treatment. In making its determination, the Internal Revenue Service will consider such factors as the purpose for which the property was held, the time resale was contemplated, the number of sales, and the amounts realized from the sales. A dealer specializing exclusively in the sale of paintings could probably prove that a sale of a statue was not in his normal course of business, i.e., selling paintings. But if this dealer were to sell a number of statues, the Internal Revenue Service would probably consider him a dealer in statues and, therefore, not eligible for capital gains treatment on the sale of these statues.

A "capital asset" held for less than six months produces what is called a short-term capital gain, which is

135

treated differently from the gain on an asset held for more than six months. On the assumption that, in the normal course of events, an art work will be held for more than six months before sale, the treatment of short-term capital gains will not be covered in this book. Should a problem arise, the Internal Revenue Service, an accountant, or a lawyer should be consulted.

A person collecting art on a large scale is likely to have other investments that may include stocks, bonds, or real estate. It is worthwhile, therefore, to explain further the statement that the capital gain tax is levied on *net* gain. Net gain is long capital gain less long-term capital losses and less net short-term capital losses. Some collectors, however, may not be able to claim offsetting losses as will be further explained below. Individuals having capital losses pay tax at the preferential basis on the year's capital gain minus capital losses—minus again the excess of short-term losses over short-term gains.

Gains from the sale or exchange of long-term capital assets are treated in the same way whether or not the asset may have been held for the production of income. Losses incurred in selling long-term capital assets are, however, treated differently. This is true even though gain from exactly the same kind of transaction would be taxable. As a general rule, losses on the sale or exchange of property are deductible only if income producing property is involved.

Art held by collectors may or may not be held as an investment; that is, to produce income. As a rule, the Internal Revenue Service would probably assume that a

136

collection was not held for investment and would, therefore, refuse any deduction claimed for losses on a sale. If a collector chooses to assert that his holdings are for investment in order to deduct losses resulting from sale, the burden of proof respecting his intention is on him. In a recent case it was held that for a collector to claim such losses, he would have to prove that he was engaged in the collection and maintenance of art objects "primarily" for investment reasons rather than for personal pleasure and enjoyment (according to the Supreme Court, "primarily" means "of first importance" or "principal" and not merely "substantial"). Proving intention, as noted earlier, is likely to be difficult.

The government's refusal to recognize losses on the sale of art works means that where some art works are sold at a gain and others at a loss during a given year, the net capital gain is simply the gain on those works that yielded a profit, not the gain minus the loss. There would be a deductible loss for someone selling art work at a gain only where the loss was on some other property held for the production of income (for example, securities or real estate).

Were it possible to convince the Internal Revenue Service that art works had been held for investment, losses on sales could be deducted from taxable income to the extent that they do not exceed capital gains. But if capital losses exceed capital gains, the extent of deductibility will be determined by allowing $1 of long-term capital loss to offset only $.50 of ordinary income. Therefore, a taxpayer will have to have long-term capital losses of $2,000 in order to use his full $1,000 annual deduction from ordinary income. Long-term capital losses that exceed the annual $1,000 deduction may be carried over to future years.

DONATION OF ART WORKS

A collector, like an artist, may choose to donate a work of art to a charity. As long as the donation is made to a charitable organization for use in its exempt function and is capital gains property, the fair market value of the piece, not its cost, as in the case of the artist who created the work, is deductible from a collector's current income. By comparison, where a dealer donates a work of art from his inventory, he may only deduct the cost or adjusted basis of the piece, and not the unrealized income component of the work. Where such a work of art has greatly appreciated in value, the collector alone is in a unique position to gain the advantage of a large tax deduction without a corresponding outlay of cash. Therefore, it is more advantageous to the collector to donate the work rather than to sell it and then contribute the cash proceeds.

Consider, for example, a painting bought by a collector for $2,000 that is now worth $10,000. If the painting is given to a museum for use in its exempt function, a charitable deduction in the amount of $10,000 may be claimed. If the painting is sold for $10,000, a capital gains tax would have to be paid, usually 25 percent, on the realized gain. In this case, the tax on the $8,000 profit would be $2,000. If the donor reduces his contribution accordingly, he will give only $8,000 cash instead of a $10,00 work of art.

138

If, instead, the collector should decide that he wants to recover a portion of his initial investment of $2,000 and still make a charitable contribution, he may sell the painting to the charity at his cost and donate the difference between the cost and the market value, claiming a charitable deduction of $8,000. This is generally referred to as a "bargain sale."

Where a taxpayer makes a bargain sale to a charity, he is treated as though he sold a part of the donated property and made a gift of the balance. In the example cited above, since the selling price of the painting ($2,000) equals 20 percent of its fair market value at the time the gift is made, the transaction is treated as a sale of 20 percent of the painting. Therefore, since the painting had a cost of $2,000, the 20 percent portion, which he "sold" for $2,000, is considered to have cost $400 (20 percent of his original cost of $2,000), resulting in a long-term capital gain of $1,600. By comparison, where a dealer sells an item from his inventory to a charity in a bargain sale for an amount equal to or in excess of his cost, he does not enjoy any charitable deduction.

For a collector, the least desirable approach, then, is to sell the work and contribute the proceeds. As between the other two methods, donation of the work results in a larger deductible contribution to the charity, while the sale of the work at cost results in the greatest after-tax cash benefit to the taxpayer. The taxpayer making a bargain sale should notify the charity that he intends to make a contribution of the excess of the fair market value of the painting over the sale proceeds. A letter accompanying the painting at the time it is transferred to the charity which sets forth the taxpayer's intent should suffice.

PERCENTAGE LIMITATIONS ON CHARITABLE DONATIONS Saving taxes has always been one of the stimuli for charitable giving. Nevertheless, the tax benefits resulting from charitable donations will depend on what type of property is contributed and the technique or method used to make the contribution.

Under the 1969 Tax Reform Act, the maximum amount of contributions an individual can deduct in any one taxable year is governed by certain percentage limitation rules. An individual is permitted a maximum deduction of 50 percent of his "contribution base" if his contribution is made to certain charities. "Contribution base" means an individual's adjusted gross income, disregarding any net operating loss carryback to the taxable year.

This 50 percent limitation applies to contributions that are made to publicly supported charities and to certain types of private foundations. These limitation rules are consistent with the general theme of the law, which favors and encourages charitable contributions to recognized public charities, but frowns on or discourages gifts to certain types of private charitable organizations.

If a taxpayer desires to maximize his charitable deduction, he must contribute to a charitable organization that qualifies for a 50 percent deduction. The 50 percent limitation applies to familiar charities such as hospitals, schools, religious groups, and government units. It also applies to certain organizations whose support comes primarily from public or governmental sources such as public museums and libraries and to certain types of private foundations such as "pass-through foundations" and "pooled-fund foundations." It will be the taxpayer's responsibility to make sure that the organization receiving his donation is a qualified 50 percent organization. All other organizations, including private foundations that do not pass their contributions through to qualified charities within specified time limits, are treated as 20 percent type organizations and allow a donor to deduct only 20 percent of his contribution base. Should a taxpayer wish to check on the extent of the deductibility of a particular contribution, he will find helpful the Treasury Department's booklet, "Cumulative List, Organizations Described in Section 170(c) of the Internal Revenue Code of 1954 . . ." which may be purchased from the Superintendent of Documents, Government Printing Office, Washington, D.C.

The 1969 Tax Reform Act increased the percentage limitation within which contributions are deductible to 50 percent of the "contribution base." However, the new rules applicable to capital gain property (such as works of art) may negate the potential benefit of the increased percentage limitation. These new rules regarding contributions of appreciated capital gain property are particularly applicable to collectors of art and are a model of complexity.

30 PERCENT LIMITATION Appreciated property means property with a fair market value that is greater than the donor's cost or adjusted basis. This is generally the case where works of renowned artists are involved. Under the new rules, if a collector contributes appreciated capital gain property (such as a piece of sculpture) to a 50 percent organization (such as a museum) for use in its exempt functions, he may deduct the full fair market value of the sculpture up to a maximum of 30 percent of his "contribution base." In this case, the 30 percent maximum is applied instead of the 50 percent maximum, which would govern if a gift of nonappreciated property or cash was made instead. Thus, any appreciation, no matter how small, makes the 30 percent limitation applicable if the recipient organization uses the gift in a manner related to its exempt purpose or function. If, on the other hand, the recipient organization does not use the gift in a related function, the donor will only be able to deduct his cost plus 50 percent of the inherent long-term gain; but here he can deduct up to 50 percent of his contribution base. The existence of a "related use" is extremely important and is discussed at length on pages 144 to 146.

In some cases, property should be first sold and then the proceeds should be contributed. This is the case where business or investment property is worth less than its cost because the charitable deduction will be the same under either a sale of the property with a donation of the sales proceeds, or a gift of the property itself. Yet by making a prior sale the taxpayer will also be able to deduct any loss incurred. A taxpayer need not consider making a prior sale in the case of property held for personal use, since a loss on such property is not deductible for tax purposes.

To further complicate the matter, a taxpayer who has

exceeded his 30 percent contribution base may elect to deduct contributions of appreciated capital gain property made to 50 percent organizations under the 50 percent limitation rather than under the 30 percent limitation. However, in order to elect a 50 percent deduction, the value of the contribution must be reduced to the extent of 50 percent of the long-term capital gain that would have been recognized if the property had been sold at fair market value. The purpose of this election is to give the taxpayer (where relatively small amounts of appreciation are involved) an opportunity to achieve approximately the same result that he would otherwise reach by selling the property and donating the proceeds to charity. Unfortunately, if the taxpayer increases his allowable percentage limitation from 30 percent to 50 percent, he will permanently lose a deduction of one-half of the long-term capital gain. However, on the plus side, unused portions of 30 percent contributions can be carried over to future years.

20 PERCENT LIMITATION If the taxpayer makes a contribution to an exempt organization that does not qualify as a 50 percent organization, his deduction will be limited to 20 percent of his "contribution base." As a rule of thumb, contributions to 20 percent organizations, such as nonoperating private foundations that do not pass contributions through to qualified charities, do not yield maximum tax benefits. This is because deductions for contributions to 20 percent organizations are allowed only to the extent of any unused portion of the 50 percent limitation, but in no case can a deduction of this type exceed 20 percent of the "contribution base." Excess contributions to 20 percent organizations will be lost forever.

A contribution of an appreciated work of art to a 20 percent private foundation organization should be avoided, since 50 percent of the amount of the appreciation in value is lost as a deduction. This reduction in the amount of the deduction achieves approximately the same tax results as would a sale of the work of art and a contribution of the proceeds.

This discussion of limitations imposed on the deduction of a charitable contribution is extremely complex. Moreover, new rules and interpretations are being issued frequently and unexpectedly. A prospective donor should review his particular situation with competent advisers to determine the probable results of donating either property or money to specific charities.

RELATED USE AND UNRELATED USE—THAT IS THE QUESTION Collectors of art that has appreciated in value have another worry—the amount of value of each contribution that can be deducted. This should be contrasted with the percentage limitations which are concerned with the total amount of contributions the taxpayer can deduct. Only certain contributions involving appreciated property are subject to valuation reduction rules because Congress undoubtedly felt that they yielded too much of a tax benefit.

Where a charitable recipient does not use the contributed property in a manner related to its exempt purpose or function, the contribution deduction is reduced by one-half of the long-term capital gain or, in other words, the contribution deduction is limited to cost plus one-half the gain. Application of this rule depends on the use made of the contributed property. The distinction is bound to cause problems for collectors. What is a related use which offers a full deduction, and an unrelated use which affords a limited deduction?

A clear case of related use is a gift of a picture or piece of sculpture to a museum that displays the piece or else places it in storage for later exhibition. A question may arise in the case of a college or university as to whether or not they are using the work of art for their exempt purpose, unless the piece is used in a course of art instruction. However, if an object of art was given to a hospital or to the United Appeal and the intention on the part of the donor and the recipient was to sell the object privately or at auction, the appreciation of the item would be taken into account in reducing the deduction taken by the donor.

If the donor anticipated that his gift was the type that would normally be used for the recipient's exempt purposes, and if the donor did not expressly contemplate the recipient selling the item, the donor should be entitled to deduct the fair market value, regardless of whether or not the exempt organization actually uses the gift as might have been expected. On the other hand, it should be obvious that if the donor and the donee agree that the donated object should be promptly sold or otherwise disposed of, the donor must deduct 50 percent of the appreciated value from his deductible contribution.

Assume, by way of example, that a collector with an adjusted gross income of $10,000 gave a painting, which he had purchased five years before for $1,000, but now

145

had a fair market value of $11,000, to a 50 percent organization. The organization did not use the painting in its tax exempt function. The amount of the taxpayer's deduction would be $6,000 or the original cost of $1,000 plus $5,000 (one-half of the long-term capital gain of $10,000). Since the taxpayer could only deduct $5,000 (or one-half of his $10,000 adjusted gross income), the $1,000 excess could be carried over for five years but would remain deductible up to 50 percent of the future taxable years' adjusted gross income.

The value placed on an appreciated work of art with a cost of $50,000 and a fair market value of $75,000, which is donated to a 50 percent organization, may be illustrated as follows:

Type of Donor	Recognized Gain If Sold	Reduction	Recognized Contribution
Collector			
(1) Put to related use	$25,000	—	$75,000
(2) Put to unrelated use	$25,000	$25,000	$62,500
Dealer	$25,000	$25,000	$50,000

VALUING A WORK OF ART Where a piece of art is sold, its value is usually the selling price. However, where an art work is donated, its value can only be estimated. In recent years, the Internal Revenue Service has looked carefully at the values set on contributed art

146

works. This has occurred because many taxpayers are inclined to exaggerate the value of such contributions. In order to counteract this raid on the U.S. Treasury, the IRS has used a panel of art dealers and other art experts, called the Art Advisory Panel, to evaluate and review appraisals used by taxpayers to support values claimed for various art objects.

In 1966 the IRS prescribed certain procedures to be followed as a guideline by all persons making appraisals of donated property. This is significant because taxpayers are required to furnish to the IRS detailed information relative to contributions of property, particularly those for which deductions in excess of $200 are claimed. If the value of the item was determined by an appraisal, the signed appraisal report must accompany the tax return. The appraisal report should contain, at a minimum, such information as the appraiser's qualifications, the appraised value along with the basis for determining that value, the date on which the property was valued, the date of the appraisal, and the signature of the appraiser. By submitting this supporting documentation, the taxpayer will minimize the chances of a costly disagreement with the IRS. As an added inducement to obtaining an appraisal, the IRS has ruled that the appraisal fee paid in determining the value of property given to a charity is deductible.

GIFT OF A FUTURE RIGHT TO POSSESS Prior to 1964, a collector could give a valuable painting, an expensive piece of sculpture, or an antique to a recognized charity and retain possession of the article during his

147

lifetime. If the charity would take possession after the donor's death, the taxpayer could claim a current income tax deduction for the current value of the future interest, as determined from life expectancy tables acceptable to the Treasury Department. By virtue of a 1964 amendment to the Internal Revenue Code, a donor is no longer eligible for a current charitable deduction if he retains during his lifetime an interest in the donated property. The charitable deduction is considered made when all rights to possession and enjoyment of the property have expired or are held by a person other than the donor.

CONTRIBUTIONS IN INSTALLMENTS Charitable deductions for the full value of art works can be obtained by giving such works in installments. The problem arises where the donor wants to give an art object whose value exceeds his limitation in any one year. If the gift were in the form of cash, the donor need only to arrange to make the contribution in installments in different tax years. But where the contribution is in the form of property, the taxpayer may give fractional ownership interests in the work. Under this plan the donor could work out a system that would call for regular fractional contributions each year up to the amount of the maximum charitable deduction allowable. Because of the newly imposed restrictions on charitable contributions where the donor retains the right of use and enjoyment, it is essential that the art work be transferred to the donee at the outset, otherwise no deduction may be taken.

148

CONCLUSION

Under our tax laws, all taxpayers are entitled to deductions for contributions made to qualifying charities. The art collector, individual as well as corporate, is in a unique position not only to gain enjoyment from his art, but also to conserve taxes. Effective planning for these savings generally requires professional advice. The collector or dealer would be shortsighted to forego legal assistance before making a charitable donation of a work of art.

Chapter 7

CUSTOMS

Works of art produced in foreign countries are frequently shipped into the United States. An American museum may be assembling a Renoir exhibition including pieces owned by foreign museums and collectors. A dealer in San Francisco may have purchased a fine piece of sculpture in France with an intention to resell in this country. An American tourist may have taken a liking to a piece of ancient Egyptian art and acquired it for display in his home. Commercial goods brought from one country to another are often subjected to tariff; most countries, however, do not place such duties on works of art. Though the United States has now joined the list of countries that do not levy a tax on works of art, our history in that area is, to say the least, somewhat embarrassing.

The Tariff Act of 1897, reversing earlier policies, had levied a 20 percent tax on all art works imported into the United States. By 1908, considerable opposition to this legislation had been generated, resulting in the organization of the Free Art League. This organization strove to modify the Tariff Act and gained a partial victory when duties were removed from works of art more than twenty years old, and reduced on other art to 15 percent. As expected, this compromise was not acceptable to the art world. The argument was advanced that free access to art of the world would cultivate public tastes and in-

150

crease the demand for the works of American artists. In light of the growth of interest in art, there is little doubt that this was a valid argument. The tariff was attacked, also, for failure to produce the anticipated revenue. Apparently the tax did not protect the American artist from foreign competition; instead it simply discouraged the importation of art into the United States.

The efforts of those individuals advocating the repeal of tariff finally met with success in 1913. In that year the duty was removed from original art works. The real problem was not solved until 1959. The problem was what, for purposes of legislation, is art? The definition of art, written into the legislation, limited the artist to the use of traditional materials, just at a time when new media were being explored. For example, is the collage (the pasting of paper and other items on canvas) a form of art? The customs law, at least, did not recognize it. The law prevented also the free entry of abstract sculpture or constructions.

Faced with problems of deciding what is art in particular cases, customs officials were bound by earlier opinions of our courts which, for certain purposes, had been asked to define art. In an 1892 case, the United States Supreme Court held that not all art was entitled to free entry, but only "free fine arts." The court defined the free fine arts as those "intended solely for ornamental purposes, and including paintings in oil and water, upon canvas, plaster, or other materials, and original statuary or marble, stone or bronze." This definition was followed in a number of later cases.

Unfortunately the collage, the piece of abstract painting and sculpture, and the construction did not comply with the judicial definition of art. The courts reasoned that Congress never intended to incorporate all beautiful and artistic objects within the duty-free range of "works of art." Rather the courts decided that "works of art" must be suggestive of natural objects as the artist sees them—*representational* in character. This rule was first successfully contested in 1928 when Constantin Brancusi's *Bird in Flight* was imported into the United States.

The *Bird in Flight* resembled a truncated propeller cast in metal. To the artist its graceful curves interpreted the flight of a bird, but the customs officers disagreed, assessed the article as a "manufacture of metal," and levied a tax on it. The decision to tax was then appealed to the Customs Court. In reversing the decision to tax, the court felt that "under the influence of modern schools of art the opinion previously held has been modified with reference to what is necessary to constitute art within the meaning of the statute." In reaching this decision, the Customs Court listened to the testimony of leading artists, sculptors, critics, and museum officials. In effect, the court took the position that it was not a judicial responsibility to decide what is art, but rather the collector of customs should rely on the opinion of art experts. The *Brancusi* case seemed to be strong authority in favor of abandoning the representational test for determining what qualifies as a work of art.

In spite of the *Brancusi* precedent, the Customs Court in 1934 retreated from its position when faced with the problem of classifying a sculptured glass vase by the French sculptor, Henri Navarre. The court observed that the designs Navarre had molded (after the glass

152

had partially solidified) did not represent anything found in nature. Although three art experts testified that the imported vases were works of art, the court held otherwise, reasoning that these particular vases could have been produced by an artisan as well as by an artist. The court admitted that the method of manufacture and the unique appearance of the vases would certainly appeal to the artistic taste of some people, but that the art style from which these vases derived was merely decorative, and "not such as has always been held to be the practice of the free fine arts." In reaching this decision, the court not only returned to the representational standard as the true criterion for a work of art, but also suggested that the article must not serve a utilitarian purpose.

The effect of the 1934 case was to force the collector of customs to make a decision concerning free entry in each individual case. The collector recognized that a work of fine art had to be representational of something in nature, but found it difficult to avoid a literal interpretation in most cases. His ultimate test was probably based on whether the particular work had a title suggesting that it was supposed to represent something found in nature. Fortunately, Congress recognized the dilemma of the customs collector and amended the Tariff Act in 1959 to encompass within the provisions for free entry most forms of artistic expression. These amendments removed many of the judicial precedents and antiquated laws that had previously placed a tax on culture. Nevertheless, recent cases draw a distinction between a work that has utilitarian value and an object of admiration and contemplation. Unless a work can be characterized as solely ornamental, it will not be entitled to free entry.

ORIGINAL WORKS

The Tariff Act amendments in 1959 modified existing provisions for importing works of the free fine arts. The new legislation contained a "catch-all" clause which empowered the collector of customs to admit duty-free, in addition to the types of work specifically enumerated, those objects proven to represent "some school, kind or medium of the free fine arts." Such proof may be required by the collector of customs from an art expert to establish the status of unprecedented works, of kinds or mediums that are not listed in the customs schedules.

Besides making the statute open ended, so as not to foreclose from the free entry status the products of new forms or methods of artistic expression, the statute had also to find a means of distinguishing originals and reproductions both in the plastic and graphic fields. The statutory language of the Tariff Act does not envision the free entry of mass-produced works of art. On the other hand, it is recognized that "sculpture" is often produced by casting in metal or bronze from artist's models, a method that allows for the production of many castings from one model. In order to prevent the free importation of Eiffel Tower paperweights, for example, the law limits the number of castings that may be entered duty-free to ten replicas plus the original model.

PRINTS AND GRAPHIC ART

Similar problems of categorization arise in the graphic field due to the advances made in techniques

154

for making original prints. The general requirements for an original print to be considered a work of art are set forth on page 113.

To qualify for duty-free entry into the United States, the customs regulations specify that an eligible work be printed by hand from plates, stones, or blocks etched, drawn, or engraved with hand tools. This requirement eliminates works of art that are produced by photochemical or other mechanical processes. As a general rule, one useful method to distinguish an original print from a reproduction is to locate the signature of the artist and the edition number of the particular print in relation to the number representing the total edition of the series. At the present time there is no limit on the number of original prints that may be entered duty-free; the limits are such as may be set by the mechanics of the process and the realities of the market place.

If the declaration to the Customs Bureau states that a print is a reproduction, the importer and anyone charged with his knowledge would be guilty of fraud if the work was later sold as an original print. Should the purchaser wish to authenticate a print before making a purchase, he should ask to examine a copy of the customs declaration.

WORKS OF ART PRODUCED BY AN AMERICAN ARTIST RESIDING TEMPORARILY ABROAD

If an American artist temporarily resides abroad and creates a work of art during his visit, he is certainly entitled to bring his art back into this country duty-free under the exemptions granted for original works or for original prints. Interestingly though, the revised tariff schedules include as a separate category works of art which are productions of American artists residing temporarily abroad. Moreover, the language of this category is broader in scope than comparable sections since the word "original" is not used in describing the works of art. It would seem, therefore, that the American artist in this circumstance may be permitted to enter duty-free more than ten castings, reproductions which are not produced completely by hand, and works that, while artistic in nature, may also have some utilitarian value. Because the apparently broad coverage of this category may be restricted in practice, it would be advisable for the artist to check with the Collector of Customs before shipping into this country works of his that might not fall under the general heading of "free fine arts."

ANTIQUES

The collector of antiques should remember that for purposes of gaining a duty-free classification, the date of production is the deciding factor. The tariff schedule lists different dates for different classes of objects.

1. Rugs and carpets may enter duty-free if produced prior to 1701.
2. Violins, violas, violoncellos, and double basses of all sizes may enter duty-free if made prior to 1801.
3. Ethnographic objects made in traditional aboriginal styles may enter duty-free if produced at least fifty years prior to their date of entry.
4. All other objects may enter duty-free if made prior to 1830.

However, if any of the foregoing duty-exempted items have been repaired with a substantial amount of additional material within three years prior to the date of importation, a duty is levied upon the value of the repairs at the rate which would apply to the article itself in its repaired condition.

Obviously, other art antiquities may include works admittable duty-free under the general definition of works of art. This overlap again raises the problem of the relative coverage of the different schedules.

STAINED GLASS WINDOWS AND TAPESTRIES

Duty-free status for stained glass windows and tapestries depends upon the value and intended use of each item. To be duty-free, the glass must be valued at $15 or more per square foot, be designed and produced by or under the direction of a professional artist, and be intended for use in a place of worship. Tapestries must be valued over $20 per square foot and must be fit only for use as wall hangings.

INTENDED USE

In addition to tariff exemptions based on the type of work, the law allows exemptions for certain intended uses. For example, where museums and other educational institutions enter what otherwise would be dutiable exhibition material, these articles are placed in a duty-free status. In certain situations, a bond must be given by the institution for the payment of lawful duties which may accrue should any of the articles be sold, transferred, or used for a purpose contrary to the provisions of the schedule authorizing duty-free admission.

157

In each case, the schedule classifies each item that may be imported for a duty-free use. Thus, the importer must establish to the satisfaction of the Customs Bureau that a certain object, which normally would be subject to a tariff, is to be used for a qualifying purpose.

EXPORT RESTRICTIONS

Before mentioning some general provisions of the United States Customs Law, the reader should recognize that while our country encourages the entry of original art, many nations control the sale and export of their art. This is done primarily to conserve national treasures. As a result, some nations require that a license be procured prior to exportation, and some nations have even reserved the right of preemption to purchase works of art which may be exported. The collector is best advised to investigate the legal restrictions before purchasing a work of art in a foreign country.

GENERAL CUSTOMS PROVISIONS

The customs laws provide a general duty-free allowance that each American resident returning from abroad may claim. United States residents are allowed to bring back $100 in duty-free merchandise based on the fair retail value instead of the wholesale value as provided in the previous law. This means that the shipper may include within his $100 general exemption any type or category of taxable art that has been purchased abroad.

A resident returning to this country must bring his purchases with him at the time of entry if they are to be included in the $100 exemption. This means that a tourist who has not used his full $100 exemption cannot order merchandise to be sent directly to his residence and then include these items in his duty-free allowance.

An institution that has been organized solely for religious, philosophical, educational, scientific, or literary purposes, or for the encouragement of the fine arts, is permitted to import, duty-free, certain goods of an educational or artistic nature. These imported goods must be used by the institution itself, or as part of a program to encourage the fine arts, and must not be for distribution, sale or commercial use. Simply because an institution is exempt from federal tax under the provisions of the Internal Revenue Code does not automatically insure it a tariff exemption unless the institution has been organized "solely" for one of the purposes specified in the tariff regulations.

DECLARATION FOR CUSTOMS

A work of art, artistic antiquity, original painting, statue, or other object must be declared for examination by a customs officer in order to gain a duty-free classification. In order to avoid a dispute at a port of entry, equipment taken out of the country by a photographer, such as cameras and lenses, should be registered with the Bureau of Customs prior to departure. There are standard declaration forms furnished by the Bureau of Customs, to be used for different types of objects or for objects entering under different conditions. Where a work of art is brought into the United States and a duty-free status is claimed, the importer must exhibit the invoice covering the particular article, unless the customs examiner is satisfied that such a statement is not necessary to a proper determination of the facts.

Chapter 8

INSURANCE

Insurance is important to the collector, the artist, and the dealer. While money will not replace a work of art damaged or destroyed, it will at least reduce or eliminate the concomitant financial loss. For the artist, his works represent an investment of time, and undoubtedly some money. If the works are lost, so is his source of future income, unless that loss is protected by insurance. For the collector, works of art may represent a considerable financial investment. If the property is lost so is a portion of the collector's personal wealth, unless the collector is covered by insurance. For the dealer, his inventory may represent a substantial investment of time and money. If his stock in trade is lost, the continuity of his business may be in jeopardy unless his inventory of art is protected by insurance. Moreover, if the dealer is holding art work on consignment, he is taking the risk that he will be liable to pay the owner for property destroyed while in his possession.

INSURANCE AS CONTRACT

An insurance policy is a form of contract, subject to the general rules of contract law. It is, however, a special type of agreement known as an "aleatory" contract. The *Concise Oxford Dictionary* defines aleatory as "depending on the throw of a die or on chance." An insurance policy is essentially a bet. The characteristic that distinguishes an aleatory from the usual bilateral contract is that one of the parties to the contract may never have to perform. Whether performance will be necessary depends solely upon the happening of an event that may never occur; the house may not burn down and the painting may not be stolen.

The laws pertaining to aleatory contracts differ in some respects from those respecting the normal bilateral contract. The tendency of the courts is to interpret the promises of each party to an aleatory contract as independent, rather than dependent. If a buyer promises to pay $1,000 for the delivery of an automobile, the buyer's duty to pay is dependent upon the car being delivered. The same contract can be drafted so that the promises are independent. For instance, the buyer promises to pay $1,000 and the seller promises to deliver a car. In that form, the buyer may have to pay regardless of whether the car is delivered, and to gain possession of the car he must go to court. The tendency of our courts, however, is to interpret nonaleatory contracts as if the promises were mutually dependent unless the independence of the promises is made absolutely clear in the agreement. In an insurance policy, however, the insurer's duty to pay upon a loss is normally held to be independent of the insured's duty to pay his premiums. If the insured misses a premium payment and then submits a claim on the policy, unless the contract provides clearly otherwise, the insurance company must pay, though the insurer may have a counterclaim for the delinquent payment.

THE FORMATION OF AN INSURANCE CONTRACT

Insurance is normally sold through agents, some of

whom are employees of the particular company and some of whom are independent agents for a number of companies. As a general rule, the agent is not authorized to bind the insurer. Instead, the agent takes the insured's application (offer) and transmits it to the company for consideration. If the company accepts the risk, it issues a policy of insurance that becomes effective upon delivery to the insured. Should the insurer issue a policy and send it to the agent for delivery to the insured, there is some difference of opinion whether that policy is effective and binding before the agent makes delivery to the customer.

There are times, however, when an agent is empowered to commit the insurer on a temporary basis. This may occur if the insured pays the premium upon the expectation of receiving coverage according to the terms of a specific policy. If the agent accepts the premium, the applicant will generally be insured until the company notifies him that his application has been rejected. It is advisable for the applicant to know whether the agent has the power to commit the insurer.

SUBJECT MATTER OF THE INSURANCE CONTRACT

Most insurance of personal property is in the form of insurance protecting all the contents of a house, without itemization. This is frequently referred to as homeowner's insurance. This would appear to be a perfectly satisfactory arrangement where no one item is of special value. Most homeowners' insurance policies only cover personal property (fine art, jewelry, furs, etc.) for up to 50 percent of the coverage on the entire

163

house. If, for example, a house is insured for $60,000, the homeowner's personal property would only be insured for a maximum of $30,000, regardless of its value. Moreover, some states have limitations on the amounts that can be paid out for certain classes of valuable items such as art works. Where one or more items are especially valuable, it is advisable that each article be appraised separately and listed in special endorsements or "floaters" to the policy. Where several items, each having considerable value, are lumped together, a problem may arise in assigning a specific value to each article. This may best be illustrated by considering the situation in which three valuable paintings are collectively insured for $50,000, and one of the paintings is destroyed. How is the value of that particular painting to be determined for insurance purposes? Or consider the situation where an auction house burns down and the house carries $1,000,000 in insurance. If the paintings in the house are owned by many different collectors, how is value to be assigned to each painting? Problems of this nature are best avoided by scheduling each item on the master policy and reporting additional items to the insurer as they are acquired.

TYPES OF INSURANCE POLICIES

Art may be insured under a variety of policies. For the casual collector, protection may be gained under a fire insurance policy. Generally fire insurance policies include such phrases as "household furniture," "household goods," "household effects," and "household property." Such phrases have been held to cover a variety of articles so long as the articles in question have been chiefly associated with the household in their general nature and use. Coverage has been denied where it appeared that the articles in question were not ordinarily associated with the household. By way of illustration, one court held that a Japanese vase was a part of the household furniture, and if not useful, constituted at least ornamental furniture. In purchasing a fire insurance policy, the assured is best advised to read the fine print carefully, and if works of art are not included within the specified coverage to discuss this matter with the agent or the insurance company.

The sophisticated collector, the gallery, the dealer, or the serious artist should purchase insurance specifically designed to protect against the destruction of art. Most companies write a "fine arts" policy; premiums for this type of insurance are very reasonable. A "fine arts" policy will generally insure against risks of loss or damage to art works which are listed in a schedule attached to the master policy. However, not all risks of loss or damage are insured, and those frequently excluded are:

1. Wear and tear, gradual deterioration, moths, vermin, inherent vice, or damage sustained due to and resulting from any repairing, restoration, or retouching process;
2. Hostile or warlike action in time of peace or war, any weapon of war employing atomic fission or radioactive force, insurrection or rebellion, seizure or destruction under quarantine or customs regulations, confiscation by order of any government or public authority;
3. Breakage of statuary, marbles, glassware, bric-a-

brac, porcelains, and similar fragile articles, unless caused by fire, lightning, aircraft, theft and/or attempted theft, tornado, windstorms, flood, earthquake, malicious damage or collision, derailment or overturn of conveyance.

Most fine arts policies also stipulate that in the event of total loss of any article or articles which are part of a set, the insurance company will pay the assured the full amount of the value of the set, but the assured must surrender the remaining article or articles of the set to the company.

Most companies will offer automatic protection for a limited period of time for new acquisitions. The consideration for this coverage is generally twofold: first, the assured will pay full premium on the acquisition from the date purchased at pro rata of the policy rate; and second, the assured will report additional items of the nature usually covered by a fine arts policy to the company within a specified number of days after the acquisition. If a new acquisition is insured under an after-acquired clause in the policy, most companies limit liability in respect to any one loss or casualty to the actual cash value of the additional item or to a maximum of 25 percent of the total amount of the policy.

Although an insurer will normally require one or more appraisals before issuing the policy, the assured and the company may fail to agree as to the amount of loss involved. Where this occurs, most fine arts policies stipulate that each party may select a competent and disinterested appraiser. The appraisers must then submit their report to an umpire (either appointed by the parties or by a court of competent jurisdiction) for a decision. The decision of the umpire may be appealed to court, but in many cases the matter is settled without going to trial.

The coverage on most fine arts policies can be adjusted by use of endorsements. Endorsements are merely attachments which become a part of the master policy, and recite the value and the amount of insurance on each scheduled item. The policy will most likely contain a clause stating that the company will not be liable for more than the amount set opposite the respective articles covered in the endorsement and that such amounts are agreed to be the values of the articles for the purpose of the policy. If a work of art appreciates in value during the effective period of the policy, it is best to so advise the company and have an amended endorsement attached to the master policy. The insurer generally includes a clause in the policy reciting that the entire policy will be void, in order to avoid inflated valuations or the misrepresentation of any material fact concerning the insurance coverage. A good idea, given the way art prices have been spiralling lately, is an inflation-guard endorsement. Some companies, in return for an additional payment of a small percentage of the regular premium, permit increased coverage on the basis of a predetermined schedule.

A few companies also offer premium discounts of up to 10 percent to the homeowner with a police-connected alarm system. This type of a policy is not widely available, but it could become more common. Even if the

167

discount is not available, having an alarm system could help convince an insurer to sell a collector added coverage.

ART WORKS ON EXHIBITION OR LOAN

There are many instances where a person other than the owner is in possession of a work. A collector may be lending a work for exhibition, he may be selling it through an agent; an artist may be doing the same. And, of course, when in transit a work is usually in the hands of another. The liability for damage to a work in any of these situations is subject to contractual agreement— whether the owner or bailee shall be liable (see discussion on page 124), the type of insurance to be provided, and who is to pay the premium.

The person with a large collection who regularly makes parts of it available to museums and the artist who regularly ships works to galleries will probably want insurance that covers their works at all times, including while in transit and in the hands of others. Those whose pieces seldom, if ever, circulate need not bother with this extra coverage; they may arrange for it on a short-term basis if the need arises.

In general, museums and galleries are likely to have blanket insurance policies covering art works they have in their possession. The difficulty of continually relisting and reappraising their exhibits is obvious, but coverage can be extended to a new work by adding endorsements to the blanket policy. The owner of the work should request certification from the insurance company that his piece has been included, by endorsement, in the master policy.

168

Where blanket coverage seems undesirable, the owner can and should make other arrangements. This is important because most fine arts policies do not cover property on the premises of any national or international exhibition unless these premises are specifically described on the policy or by endorsement. The big point with insurance is to be certain what type of coverage is wanted, which will vary from individual to individual, and to make sure that what is needed is, indeed, provided.

LOSS OR DESTRUCTION OF ART WORK

If works of art are fully insured under the provisions of an effective policy, the cost of the damage or loss will be borne by the insurance company. This does not mean, however, that the owner of an art work may insure his possession with more than one insurance company and expect to collect the full value of the lost or damaged article from each insurer. Most fine arts policies specify that if there is other insurance on the property at the time of loss, the insurer will be liable only in proportion to that insurer's share of all insurance on the property. In this way, insurance companies seek to protect themselves from excessive payouts.

The Internal Revenue Code provides that an individual taxpayer may deduct certain losses not compensated for by insurance or otherwise. The deduction is limited to losses incurred in a trade or business, losses incurred in any transaction entered into for profit, and any losses arising from fire, shipwreck, or other casualty. If the loss involves *business* property, the difference between the value of the property immediately preceding the

169

casualty and its value immediately thereafter may be deducted. A loss of a *personal* asset (not used for business or profit), however, is deductible only to the extent that each such loss exceeds $100. Moreover, there must be a sudden, unexpected, or unusual cause which precipitates the loss, rather than a gradual deterioration. It has been held that damages to personal assets by a flood, a bursting boiler, an act of vandalism, or a "sonic boom" are proper allowances.

In order to substantiate a loss for income tax purposes, the taxpayer must submit evidence in support of the cost or other basis of the property. In one case where the taxpayer could not prove the basis for a painting given to him, he was denied full recovery, but he had spent $100 to have the picture cleaned and prepared for sale; the Tax Court held that since the transaction was entered into for profit, the sum of $100 could be deducted as a loss.

Chapter 9

MUSEUMS

The art museum is a relatively new institution in our society. A great majority of art museums originated during the twentieth century. Until the emergence of art museums, public exposure to art works was very limited. Art treasures were owned primarily by private collectors, wealthy patrons, and the church.

Art museums not only collect and preserve art works, but they also educate the public. Most art museums offer guided tours and many museums conduct organized college courses and periodic lectures.

Most museums are financed by donations from individuals and from the government. Private individuals also donate large numbers of art works to museums. The federal government has stimulated donations by giving favorable tax treatment to these donations.

Management of the numerous art works in its collection poses a serious problem for many museums. Individual donors often attempt to restrict the use or sale of donated works. Frequently, museums disregard donor restrictions and dispose of these donated works without informing either the donor or the public at large.

ACQUIRING WORKS OF ART
One of the major functions of a museum is to collect and preserve cultural property. In negotiating to acquire objects of art, museum personnel, like other serious collectors, should only deal with sellers or donors who

have valid legal title to the specific work of art. Unfortunately, museums have no real way of knowing whether they are dealing in stolen or missing property unless the theft or disappearance has been widely publicized. Therefore, it is recommended that museums should not make acquisitions unless a pedigree is furnished; that is, information about the different owners of the object, the place of origin, export approvals (if applicable), and other appropriate data.

Museums are often tempted to acquire an archaeological or ethnographic object that must be exported from its country of origin. Consequently, over the years, museums have found themselves in possession of important objects belonging to the cultural heritage of other nations. In response to a common need to preserve their own heritages, some nations prohibit the export of cultural property unless an export certificate is first obtained from the government (see discussion of customs on page 158). In some countries individuals who knowingly acquire illegally exported cultural property may become subject to criminal prosecution. As a further deterrent to the illicit traffic of art objects in the international art market, many museums have agreed to abstain from purchasing and accepting donations of art which have been exported without permission from their countries of origin.

DISPOSING OF WORKS OF ART

Can a museum dispose of works in its collection? If so, may the officers and trustees of the museum sell or exchange these works at their own discretion?

These questions arose when New York's Metropolitan

Museum of Art sold a number of major works of art in private transactions. These controversial private sales forced the trustees of this museum to reassess their public responsibility in connection with both the acquisition and disposal of works of art. As a result, the old doctrine of privileged secrecy has been discarded in favor of public disclosure of how the museum buys and sells. Not only did the Metropolitan Museum pledge to issue full annual reports documenting all of its trading and selling activities, but it also agreed that all future cash sales of art objects valued at more than $5,000 will be made at public auction, unless the sale is to a museum or similar institution; that no work valued at more than $10,000 will be disposed of within twenty-five years after its receipt if the donor or his heirs object; that at least forty-five days public notice will be given prior to disposing of any work of art which has been displayed in the museum within the last ten years and is valued at more than $25,000; and that if any work valued at more than $5,000 is being considered for sale, the attorney general will be notified in advance of any restrictions which may have been placed upon disposition by the original donor. This policy may soon become a standard operating practice for other museums as well.

LICENSING AGREEMENTS

Museums are frequently approached by commercial firms who are interested in reproducing and marketing works of art from a museum's collection. Such items as antique jewelry, historic coins, native handicrafts, ceremonial masks, and the like make worthwhile souvenirs and valued gifts. Reproducing objects from the museum's collection can be a real benefit to a museum since this offers a means of generating additional revenues and expands the educational and cultural impact of the museum. However, when museums contemplate such business ventures, they must exercise care to insure that revenues will indeed be produced, good products will reach the marketplace, and the overall reputation of the museum will be enhanced.

In order to control the production and marketing of an object by a third party, the museum should carefully define the rights and responsibilities of the party through a licensing agreement. Museums should not sign licensing agreements in haste. At the outset, the firm who will produce and market the item, known as the licensee, should be screened to insure that it has the requisite financial stability, an effective channel of distribution, the ability to create a quality product, and a reputation for fair dealing within its industry. Assuming that the licensee meets these qualifications, the museum, as the licensor, must determine whether it possesses the basic legal rights to the particular object to permit the granting of a license. For example, if the creator of the object retained any rights in his work, or the donor of the object restricted its reproduction or use, the museum may not be in a position to offer an effective license. Then, too, the museum must resolve any questions concerning the extent to which it can lawfully permit objects within its collection to be exploited for commercial purposes.

If a museum has the power to license the production and marketing of an object, and its tax-exempt status will not be jeopardized (see page 182), a written agreement should be prepared in order to avoid potential misunderstandings. In the agreement, the museum should try to limit the rights granted to the absolute minimum necessary for the licensee to carry out the project. The length of the agreement and the territorial extent of the licensee's rights, if any, should be clearly defined, as well as any options to renew or any conditions upon which renewal are based. Obviously, if the licensee breaches the agreement or fails to meet certain standards of performance, the museum should retain the right to terminate the license prematurely.

Objects of art are often difficult and expensive to duplicate. Prior to entering a licensing agreement, the parties should decide which one will be responsible for costs incurred in manufacturing and promoting the project. If possible, a museum should ask that the licensee absorb any start-up costs even though the program may not ultimately prove a financial success. Even if the licensee agrees to assume these initial costs, the museum should retain the right to approve the item at various stages of its design and manufacturing process. This is especially important where an item is being produced that will be marketed under the name of the museum.

Most licensing agreements provide that the museum is to receive a royalty based on a percentage of sales. But since "sales" may not mean the same thing to each party, it is recommended that the term "sales" be defined in advance. Some museums find it easier to compute royalties on gross sales, while others prefer net sales, which allow for the deduction of certain costs and overhead incurred by the licensee. The agreement should also include the right to inspect the licensee's books to assure that royalties are being faithfully disbursed. Where possible, a museum should insist that the licensee guarantee a minimum royalty. This should stimulate the licensee to use its best efforts to perform.

Care should be exercised in drafting the agreement so that the museum and the licensee will not be deemed partners. As a partner, the museum will be exposed to liability for acts of the licensee over which the museum has no control. For further protection, the museum should preclude the licensee from selling or assigning its rights in the licensing agreement to a third party without prior written consent of the museum. This restriction on assignability will allow the museum to control the identity of the licensee during the period of the agreement.

But regardless of how thoroughly the parties have negotiated prior to signing the license agreement, it is reasonable to expect that some misunderstanding may arise. If this occurs, it is advantageous for the parties to agree to arbitrate in order to reach a speedy resolution of their dispute. Lawsuits are not only expensive and time-consuming, but they often generate unfavorable publicity.

INSURING THE COLLECTION

Museums, with their art treasures, are storehouses of enormous cultural wealth. It is evident that no amount of insurance could replace a damaged Rembrandt, but insurance could, in the event of tragedy, help to procure a comparable work.

Museums insure their collections under a variety of

arrangements. Many museums have multiple policies to avoid the high cost of one all-encompassing blanket policy. This insurance portfolio consists of two or more policies: a minor policy for coverage up to a fixed amount to insure against pilfering, breakage, etc., and a major policy to cover any disaster (fire, flood, or other extraordinary loss) extending from the limits of the minor policy. Some of the more affluent museums carry no insurance, choosing to cover any losses from their own treasuries.

Many very expensive individual art works are usually insured under their own policies. This must be done because famous and rare works, as a matter of courtesy, often are loaned for exhibition to other museums and the donating museum's blanket insurance policy will usually only cover items within the museum. Another reason for special coverage of major works involves the problem of determining specific value in the event of loss or damage.

EXHIBITIONS AND LOANS

Great loan exhibitions, each illustrating by a selection of the very finest examples the work of a single master or a single country or a single period, serve a wide range of useful purposes.

To many art students and to most ordinary citizens great exhibitions have proven to be an experience of the richest quality and a lifetime memory. Some of these exhibitions have become international events and none of them would have been possible without the cooperation of museums (and also of private collectors) in many countries.

Before a museum can loan a work acquired through a gift, it must be determined that there were no lending restrictions imposed at the time of the donation. Regardless of whether or not specific restrictions exist, some critics claim that museums have no right to lend pictures and other works of art, which are in their charge, to other museums. Is it fair for people to go to particular museums in the expectation of seeing a particular work, only to find that it is on loan to another museum? Everyone seems to be in agreement, however, that it is dangerous for old pictures, particularly those painted on wood, to be subjected to frequent changes of temperature and humidity or to be jarred or shaken in transit.

Insurance coverage of a work at an exhibition and in transit to and from the exhibition will usually be provided by the host museum. Optionally, donors can insure their art works themselves, in which case the host museum will reimburse for the insurance expense (see discussion of insurance on page 168 and Appendix XIX Museum Loan Form).

Valuation of works loaned for exhibitions is always a problem. For insurance purposes, the donor is requested to submit his own appraisal of value, which is sometimes excessive. Where the donor's appraisal is found to be unreasonable, the museum might request another valuation or withdraw its request for a loan of the particular piece.

SECURITY PROCEDURES

In addition to procuring insurance, a museum may also employ security guards to protect its works of art against pilferage. Although these guards may serve a variety of functions, unlike public police, they are primarily oriented toward prevention and protection rather than general law enforcement. In view of this difference in function, a question is likely to arise as to the extent of power that private police are authorized to exercise. Are these powers analogous to those of public policemen, or are they limited to those of the private citizen?

Every citizen possesses certain powers of arrest, search and seizure, and self-defense. These powers are equally enjoyed by private policemen. Yet the question remains as to whether private police may legally exercise greater powers than those granted to citizens generally. Although most states require licenses for certain private police activities, these licenses generally confer no additional powers. The result is that in most states, private police possess no powers beyond those of the ordinary citizen. Some states and municipalities, however, do vest private police with the powers of public officers if certain prerequisites are satisfied.

The significance of the distinction between private and public police becomes apparent when the use of "deadly force" is contemplated to prevent the theft of a work of art. In general, an individual may use deadly force only if he "reasonably believes" his life is in danger. A public policeman may also employ such force in a number of additional settings. These situations are specifically defined by state law; consequently, the relevant state statutes must be consulted. A museum should seek the advice of a competent attorney if the employment of security guards is contemplated.

179

AUTHENTICATING WORKS OF ART

One of the most important assets of a museum is its specialized staff. Many of the art world's foremost experts serve as curators in various museums. These experts make recommendations as to acquisitions of art works and utilize their knowledge in settling questions of authenticity. As a public service, some museums allow their curators, with the aid of museum equipment, to make authentication determinations for private collectors. Without this service, few private collectors could afford the sophisticated equipment or the cost of hiring an art expert to determine a particular art work's authenticity.

Because this service is frequently provided without cost to the collector (frequently a prospective buyer), the collector should agree in writing to release the museum from any liability which might arise from its rendering of an opinion (see Appendix XV). More specifically, this agreement should contain the following provisions:

(a) An agreement that the opinion shall not be made the basis of any lawsuit against the museum or any staff member;

(b) A release from all claims upon which a lawsuit may be based;

(c) An agreement to indemnify and protect the museum and every member of its staff from any damages or expenses that may be sustained as the result of rendering an opinion.

In addition, the collector should agree that while the work of art is in the possession of the museum, the risk of loss or damage to the work shall remain with the buyer.

TAXATION

The law enumerates various categories of organizations that are exempt from income taxes. Principally, these include specified types of nonprofit groups such as charitable, religious, and educational institutions. Because museums are regarded as educational institutions, they are accorded tax-exempt treatment under the Internal Revenue Code.

An organization is not automatically exempt from tax, however, merely because it meets the requirements of the code. As a matter of fact, an income tax return must be filed until the exemption is established. To claim the exemption, an application should be filed with the district director for the district in which the museum is located. At that time, a claim for refund should also be filed since an exemption is effective as of the date of formation if the statutory requirements were met at that time.

The Internal Revenue Code also contains two additional filing requirements for organizations claiming tax-exempt status. The first, applicable only to organizations created after October 9, 1969, required notification to the Internal Revenue Service that they are applying for recognition of exempt status. In addition, all organizations, regardless of whether or not they were in existence on October 9, 1969, must notify the Internal Revenue Service that they are not private foundations. Generally, the filing of a completed Form 1023 with an attached statement indicating nonprivate foundation status will satisfy all the above requirements.

After the exemption has been established, the organization must, nevertheless, file an annual information return on Form 990; that is, a yearly statement of gross income receipts, contributions, and the like. Institutions whose gross receipts in each taxable year are normally not more than $5,000 are not required to file annual returns or to comply with the notification requirements discussed in the preceding paragraph.

Although an organization may gain tax-exempt status, it may become subject to an income tax on "unrelated business income"; that is, income from a source or business venture not substantially related to the purpose for which it received its exemption. Museums may, however, generate some revenue, while at the same time carrying out their educational purposes. The Internal Revenue Service has ruled that the rental or sale of reproductions and even greeting cards displaying reproductions contribute importantly to the museum's exempt educational purpose and, therefore, do not constitute unrelated business income. This conclusion is based on the premise that the sale of these reproductions enhances public awareness, interest, and appreciation of art. The IRS has also found, however, that the sale of scientific books and souvenirs relating to the city where the museum is located does not fall within this classification. These items, it has been concluded, have no causal relationship to art or artistic endeavor, and their sale is, therefore, unrelated to the museum's tax-exempt purpose.

It must be emphasized that this discussion is merely

182

intended to point up the various sections that may be relevant to obtaining and preserving tax-exempt status. It is by no means exhaustive, and should not be regarded as a complete guide to obtaining and maintaining a tax exemption.

LABOR RELATIONS

Frequently a museum is confronted with problems involving employees' wages, hours, and conditions of employment. A question may then arise as to whether a museum should deal with its employees collectively or on an individual basis. In certain circumstances, which will be discussed below, a duty to bargain collectively will be imposed on an employer under the National Labor Relations Act (NLRA). Before examining these situations, however, a brief introduction to the law will be helpful.

The National Labor Relations Act, which is administered by the National Labor Relations Board, covers the rights of employees to bargain collectively with their employers through representatives of their own choosing. To ensure that employees can freely choose their own representatives for the purpose of collective bargaining, the act establishes a procedure by which they can exercise their choice at a secret ballot election conducted by the National Labor Relations Board. Further, to protect the rights of employees and employers and to prevent labor disputes that would adversely affect the rights of the public, Congress has defined certain practices of employers and unions as unfair labor practices.

The power of Congress to regulate labor-management

relations is limited by the Commerce Clause of the United States Constitution. Although it can declare generally what the rights of employees are or should be, Congress can make its declaration of rights effective only in respect to enterprises whose operations "affect commerce" and labor disputes that "affect commerce." The NLRB, therefore, can direct elections and certify the results only in the case of an employer whose operations affect commerce. Similarly, it can act to prevent unfair labor practices only in cases involving labor disputes that affect, or would affect, commerce.

The term "affect commerce" is very broadly construed. The mere crossing of state lines by visitors to the museum may be sufficient to satisfy this test. Consequently, the authority of the NLRB could extend to all but purely local institutions. As a result, unless the board finds that the effect on commerce is substantial, it will probably conclude that a particular labor dispute is not of sufficient significance to justify spending government time and money in preventing or resolving the dispute. The amount of the annual gross revenue of the museum from all sources is a highly relevant consideration in this determination. If this sum exceeds $1,000,000, the likelihood of intervention by the NLRB is greatly increased.

A significant development has been the decision of the National Labor Relations Board to enter the field of private, nonprofit educational institutions. Accordingly, in some recent cases involving museums that also provide programs of art instruction, the NLRB has found that the museum, in its capacity as an employer, is required to bargain collectively with its employees. No uniform standards have been set forth to determine when

184

this duty to bargain will be imposed. This determination is dependent upon whether the operations of the institutions are of sufficient magnitude to substantially "affect commerce."

Consequently, whether a particular museum will be subject to the NLRB will most probably be decided on a case-by-case basis. The purpose of this section is merely to apprise the museum of the possibility that it will be required to bargain collectively with its employees.

EPILOGUE

I hope that by the time the artist is finished reading this book he is willing to agree with me that the law is fascinating, even if it concerns itself at times with human cupidity, arrogance, and double-dealing. But even if a taste of the law leaves bitter aftereffects, it is a form of preventive medicine that the artist will find useful in keeping him out of court, assuring that he is paid, and keeping as friends those with whom he does business.

A letter written by Michelangelo in 1542, which is reproduced below, is proof enough that the legal implications of an artist's activities are not peculiar to the twentieth century.

From Rome,
(October . . . . , 1542)

To Messer Luigi del Riccio.

Messer Luigi, Dear Friend,—Messer Pier Giovanni has been persistently urging me to begin the painting (in the Pauline Chapel). It may readily be seen, however, that this is impossible for the next four to six days, as the plaster is not yet sufficiently dry for me to begin operations. But there is another thing that vexes me far more than the plaster, some-

thing that prevents me from living, to say nothing of painting—I mean the delay in drawing up the ratification setting aside the contracts. I feel that I have been cheated, and as a result I am in a state of desperation. I have wrung from my heart 1,400 crowns which would have enabled me to work for seven years, during which I could have made two tombs, let alone one: and I only did so that I might obtain peace and be free to serve the Pope with my whole heart. Now I find myself deprived of the money and face to face with more troubles and anxieties than ever. I did what I did about the money because the Duke (of Urbino) agreed to it, and in order to get the ratification drawn up: now that I have paid the money I cannot obtain the ratification, so that it is easy to guess what all this means without my having to write it down. Enough; it is only what I deserve for having believed in other people for thirty years and for having placed myself freely at their service: painting, sculpture, hard work and too much faith have ruined me, and everything goes from bad to worse. How much better it would have been if in my early days I had been set to make sulphur matches, for then I should not have all this anxiety! I write this to vostra Signoria because, as one who wishes me well and who knows all about the matter and therefore knows the truth, you can inform the Pope what is happening, and then he may perhaps understand that I can not live, much less paint. If I had promised to begin the work, it was in the expectation of receiving the said ratification, which ought to have been given to me a month ago. I will not support this burden any longer, nor will I submit to be abused and called a swindler by those who have robbed me of life and honor. Only death or the Pope can save me now from my troubles.

Your Michelagniolo Buonarroti

Reproduced from Michelangelo,
*translated and edited by Robert W. Carden.
Houghton Mifflin Company (1913).*

APPENDIX I

AGREEMENT WITH A PRINTMAKER

THIS AGREEMENT made and entered into this _____ day of _____, 19_____, by and between _____, residing at _____, City of _____, State of _____ (hereinafter referred to as the "Artist") and _____, with offices at _____, (hereinafter referred to as the "Publisher"),

WHEREAS, the Publisher is in the business of printing, publishing, promoting, distributing and selling original signed lithographs, and

WHEREAS, the Publisher desires to have the Artist prepare and produce certain plates (insert "stones" throughout, if applicable) for such lithographs, and

WHEREAS, the Artist is willing to engage Publisher on the terms and conditions herein set forth.

NOW, THEREFORE, it is hereby agreed by and between the parties as follows:

1. The Artist shall design and execute plates for a set of _____ original lithographs for printing and publication by the Publisher. The subject matter of the lithographs shall be _____. The lithographs shall measure _____ inches by _____ inches, shall be in _____ colors, and shall be serially numbered and signed by the Artist. They shall be issued by the Publisher in a limited edition of _____ sets, each of which will be sold for a retail price of $_____.

2. The Artist shall design and execute the plates for the aforesaid lithographs in his studio or at the Publisher's premises, and shall begin work not later than _____ and shall complete the same not later than _____.

3. The Publisher shall provide all the necessary plates, working space, equipment, materials and technical assistance, all without cost to the Artist. The Artist shall be available to consult with Publisher in the event problems are encountered in the course of production, to examine successive trial proofs, to make such corrections in the plates as may be necessary, and to sign the final

prints. All artistic questions pertaining to the lithographs shall be decided by the Artist.

4. Prior to the printing of each of the lithographs in the set, the Artist's approval shall be required for the final trial proof thereof. Such approval shall be deemed to have been given when the Artist signs each such final trial proof.

5. Upon the Artist's approval of the final trial proofs, the Publisher shall print the lithographs. No more than _____ impressions shall be printed from the plate for each lithograph. Prints shall be of high quality and in conformity with final trial proofs, and upon completion, the Artist shall affix his signature to each of the lithographs in each set.

6. The Publisher shall register each lithograph in each set for copyright in the Artist's name in the United States Copyright Office; and Publisher shall affix the necessary copyright notice to each lithograph published by it. The ownership of the copyrights shall at all times reside in the Artist.

7. Upon the completion of the edition, the Publisher shall efface the plates so that the images thereon will be no longer suitable for making lithographic impressions. The Publisher shall furnish to the Artist a cancellation proof of each plate within _____ days after the completion of the edition.

8. As compensation for the work done and rights granted by the Artist hereunder, the Publisher shall furnish to the Artist, without charge, _____ sets of lithographs and shall pay the Artist the sum of $_____ as follows:
   (a) The sum of $_____ upon the execution hereof;
   (b) The sum of $_____ when the Artist approves the proof for printing; and
   (c) The sum of $_____ when the Artist signs all the lithographs in the edition.

9. The Publisher shall promote the sale of the lithographs in a dignified manner in keeping with the Artist's reputation and professional standing.

10. The Publisher's rights hereunder shall be exclusive to it only insofar as the contemplated edition of the litho-

graphs is concerned. The Artist shall be free at all times to prepare art work of every kind for others if he so desires; and the preparation of such art work shall not be deemed to contravene this Agreement.

11. Upon the sale or other disposition of the edition of the _____sets by the Publisher, this Agreement shall terminate, and all rights herein granted by the Artist to the Publisher shall revert to the Artist.

12. This Agreement shall not be assignable by any act of the Publisher or by operation of law.

13. This Agreement constitutes the entire agreement of the parties, and shall not be subject to modification except in writing duly signed by both parties.

IN WITNESS WHEREOF the parties have executed this Agreement on the day and year first written above.

_____
Publisher

_____
Artist

APPENDIX II

CONSIGNMENT SALE FORM

ABC Galleries, Inc.
New York, New York

You hereby acknowledge receipt of the following oil painting created by me:

[Name of painting—size (height and width)] (the "Painting") which Painting is consigned to you at the following price: $_____.

The purchase price of the Painting less your commission of _____% shall be delivered by you to me within _____ days from and after the date on which delivery shall be made by you under any sale or contract of sale. Title to, and a security interest in, the Painting (and any proceeds thereof) is reserved in me until sale of the Painting by you, whereupon the proceeds of such sale shall be held for me and delivered (except for such commission set forth above) to me as herein provided.

In the event of any default by you, I shall have all of the rights of a secured party under the Uniform Commercial Code.

Notwithstanding the foregoing, at any time prior to any sale of the Painting by you, at my request you will deliver the Painting to me immediately upon receipt of any instructions from me.

_____
                                    Artist

The foregoing is confirmed and
agreed to: ABC Galleries, Inc.
By _____

APPENDIX III

CONTRACTS BETWEEN MATISSE AND BERNHEIM-JEUNE

FIRST CONTRACT 1909-1912
AGREEMENT MATISSE—BERNHEIM

Between Mr. Henri-Matisse (42, route de Clamart at Issyles-Moulineaux, Seine) and Messrs. Bernheim-Jeune (15 rue Richepanse, Paris) the following has been agreed:

ART. I—All pictures of the below-mentioned sizes and intermediate sizes which Mr. Henri-Matisse executes before the fifteenth of September 1912 he agrees to sell to Messrs. Bernheim-Jeune, and they agree to buy them from him, regardless of what the subject is, at the following prices:

Format 50 Fig.—1,875 frs.
40 Fig.—1,650 "
30 Fig.—1,500 "
25 Fig.—1,275 "
20 Fig.—1,125 "
15 Fig.— 900 "
12 Fig.— 750 "
10 Fig.— 600 "
8 Fig.— 525 "
6 Fig.— 450 "

The prices of the pictures of intermediate sizes (formats *"paysage"* and *"marine"* and irregular formats) shall be in proportion to their surface and the above prices.

ART. II—In addition Mr. Henri-Matisse shall receive twenty-five percent of the profit obtained on the sale of the pictures.

ART. III—In the event that Mr. Henri-Matisse sells a certain picture while it is being painted, the difference between the above-mentioned prices and the sales prices shall be shared fifty-fifty by him and Messrs. Bernheim-Jeune.

193

ART. IV—If Messrs. Bernheim-Jeune leave in storage with Mr. Henri-Matisse a finished painting and he sells this picture directly, the profit shall also be shared fifty-fifty.

ART. V—The sales price of pictures sold by Mr. Henri-Matisse under the conditions outlined in Articles III and IV shall be no less than about double the prices indicated in Article I.

ART. VI—Paintings which Mr. Henri-Matisse himself considers sketches shall not be covered by Article I or the following Articles. Those sketches which he intends to bring into circulation shall, however, be submitted to Messrs. Bernheim-Jeune and a separate arrangement can be made for each one of them. In case no friendly understanding can be worked out, Messrs. Bernheim-Jeune shall have the right but not the obligation to acquire the sketch as outright owners at the rates set forth in Article I.

ART. VII—As soon as Mr. Henri-Matisse has finished a picture he notifies Messrs. Bernheim-Jeune. When delivering a painting he gives them information regarding any negotiations he might have had about the picture.

ART. VIII—Neither Article I nor any of the following Articles is retroactive with respect to pictures which have been commissioned before this agreement, namely: his *Self Portrait*, two canvases of 50, a landscape of 20, two canvases of about 40.

ART. IX—Mr. Henri-Matisse is free to accept, without any compensation being due to Messrs. Bernheim-Jeune, firm orders for portraits or decorations which he receives directly. Decorations will be construed only as paintings of irregular size, the dimensions of which are strictly determined by the architecture of the place where they are to be installed.

ART. X—Messrs. Bernheim-Jeune will receive twenty-five percent on the orders for decorations and portraits which Mr. Henri-Matisse accepts through them as intermediaries.

ART. XI—Upon payment of a forfeiture of 30,000 francs and a simple statement in writing addressed to the other party, each one of the contracting parties has the right at any time to cancel this agreement for the remainder of the time it is to be in force.

ART. XII—In the event that Messrs. Bernheim-Jeune pay to Mr. Matisse the forfeiture of 30,000 francs as set forth in the previous Article, Mr. Henri-Matisse shall lose all claim to the profit ultimately to be derived by Messrs. Bernheim-Jeune from the sale of the pictures which they may have in storage at the time of the abovementioned payment.

ART. XIII—This agreement has not been registered. If under any circumstances one of the contracting parties finds it advisable to have it registered, this party will assume the costs of registration.

Done in Paris, in two copies, the eighteenth of September 1909.

/s/ Henri-Matisse

SECOND CONTRACT 1912-1915

The second contract, September 18, 1912 to September 15, 1915, is virtually the same as the first except for Article V:

ART. V—The sales price of pictures sold by Mr. Henri-Matisse under the conditions outlined in Article III and IV, shall be no less than about double the prices indicated in Article I. This clause is not reciprocal with regard to Messrs. Bernheim-Jeune, who of course try to sell the pictures of Mr. Henri-Matisse in the best interest of both parties. In exceptional cases they will be free to sell at prices considerably below twice the purchase price pictures which they have offered in vain for a considerable time to collectors; or if the purchaser is another art dealer, or if a reduction in prices might attract new customers to the art of Mr. Henri-Matisse.

THIRD CONTRACT 1917-1920

The third contract was in the form of a letter from Matisse to Bernheim-Jeune, dated Paris, October 19, 1917 (*two* years and more after the expiration of the second contract). The principal paragraphs follow:

I. During the three years beginning September 19, 1917, I agree to sell to you and you agree to buy from me one-half of my production of pictures between the formats 80 to 4 inclusive and at the prices mentioned below:

FORMATS	PRICE	FORMATS	PRICE
80	6,000 frs.	15	2,500 frs.
60	5,000 "	12	2,000 "
50	4,500 "	10	1,800 "
40	4,000 "	8	1,500 "
30	3,500 "	6	1,200 "
25	3,000 "	5	1,000 "
20	2,800 "	4	800 "

II. I agree not to sell to any third party, dealers or collectors, any picture which is in the process of being painted.

III. The division mentioned in Article I shall be handled as follows: I shall advise you each time a pair of canvasses of equal or similar size is ready, and each time we shall draw lots for first choice.

IV. As far as my half of the pictures is concerned I agree not to sell any of them to any other dealers at less than the above prices marked up by thirty percent. If, however, the whole lot is sold the mark-up may be reduced to twenty percent. You, however, agree not to sell to any other dealer any of the paintings in your half at a price which is not at least forty percent above your purchase price.

V. Whether I receive these commissions [for decorations, portraits, easel paintings] directly or through your interven-

196

tion, they will count toward my half if they fall within the sizes defined in Article I.

From *Matisse: His Art and His Public* by Alfred H. Barr, Jr., Copyright 1951 by the Museum of Modern Art, New York, and reprinted with its permission.

APPENDIX IV

ARTISTS EQUITY
ARTIST—DEALER FORM OF CONTRACT

1. The _____ Gallery (address) referred to hereafter as "The Gallery" agrees to act as sales representative for _____ referred to hereafter as "The Artist" for a period of _____ year(s) from date.

2. This contract may be cancelled by either party on written notice after _____ days (or) after the end of the exhibition season in which the contract is cancelled, to be considered as _____ date.

COMMISSION

*3. The Gallery shall receive _____ percent of all sales made on its premises.

*4. The Gallery shall receive _____ percent of any portrait, sculpture or mural commissions it gets for the Artist and _____ percent of any others awarded during the period of the contract.

*5. Commissions on purchase prices shall be calculated at _____ percent of the regular gallery list price.

*6. The Gallery shall receive _____ percent of any sales made by the artist personally, without the assistance of the Gallery, provided, however, that no commission shall be paid on any sales referred to in this paragraph, unless the dealer makes sales in the contract year of at least $_____ for the artist.

*7A. The Gallery shall not receive any commissions on royalties, sale of reproduction rights or commercial assignments unless arranged by the Gallery, in which case the commission will be _____ percent. The Gallery shall receive _____ percent on works of fine art which it sells for commercial use. It shall be understood that all sales are made exclusive of reproduction rights, and written acknowledgement of that fact shall be obtained from purchaser by the Gallery. Reproduction rights may be specifically purchased with the Artist's written consent in each case.

7B. The Gallery shall not receive commissions on prizes or awards granted to the Artist by art institutions, museums, foundations or a government agency.

8. Materials, installation and foundry costs on sculpture and murals shall be deducted before calculating commissions.

9. That the Gallery promptly return all works of art, which are the property of the Artist, promptly on termination of the *contract*.

JURISDICTION
10. During the period of the contract the Artist shall not contract for any other representation except in the following fields:

. . . local representation outside the city in which the Gallery is located
. . . foreign countries
. . . other (i.e., print galleries)

The Gallery may arrange for representation of the Artist by another agency in any field reserved to it by this contract, but must arrange to pay such agency by splitting its own commission, with no added charge to the Artist.

11. In addition to continuous sales representation during the term of this agreement, work of the Artist will be exhibited in the Gallery:

a) in a one-man show of _____ weeks duration at least once every _____ years. Said show shall not be at the same time as any other one-man show in the Gallery.
b) at least one work will appear in a permanent exhibition of the Gallery Group.
c) at least one work will be exhibited in all gallery group shows of which there will be at least _____ every year.

12. Storage space will be provided at the Gallery for at least _____ works.

*13. The Artists will receive the following opportunities to cooperate in formulating the policy of the Gallery.
*See Instruction Sheet

EXPENSES

*14. When the Artist has a one-man show at the Gallery, all related costs will be borne by the Gallery.

15. The Gallery will meet expenses of packing and shipping work sent to clients and exhibitions.

*16. The Gallery will insure all work in its possession against loss and damage up to ——————— percent of sale price.

FINANCES

*17. The Artist and the Gallery will agree in writing on prices for all work in the possession of the Gallery. The Gallery may not accept a lower offer without the Artist's consent in writing.

18. All works are received by the Gallery on consignment and in trust. All sums received by the Gallery on account of works sold are received in trust and the net proceeds, after deduction of commission and expenses agreed to be chargeable to the Artist, shall be immediately deposited in a special trust bank account and there retained until paid out to the Artist.

19A. The Gallery will pay the Artist promptly on or before the 15th of each month the amount due him from any sale made in the previous month, regardless of any arrangement the Gallery may make with the client for deferred payment or financing of the sale. The Artist's consent to participate in each case must be obtained in writing.

OR

19B. The Gallery will pay the Artist $——————— per month for the period of the contract, which shall be minimum compensation. The Artist will receive a quarterly statement of his account, and will be paid any excess of Artist's share of sales over his monthly allowance at the end of each year of the contract.

200

*20. The Gallery will set up a welfare fund consisting of _____ percent on each sale contributed by the Artist and _____ percent by the Gallery.

21. A Standard Artists Equity receipt will be given the Artist for all work received and he must acknowledge in writing all work returned.

22. Annual statements in writing covering sales, receipts, payments to the Artist and all other matters, together with a list of work on hand, will be furnished by the Gallery within thirty (30) days after the end of each year of the term hereof. The Gallery shall keep adequate records of all its transactions with respect to each Artist's work, which records shall be available for inspection during the regular business hours by the Artist or his representative authorized in writing.

23. FURTHER ARRANGEMENTS:

. . . .
Date

. . . .
For the Gallery

. . . .
For the Artist

. . . .
Witness

*See Instruction Sheet

201

ARTISTS EQUITY
STANDARD RECEIPT FORM

Received from ....
Name of Artist

Address .... Phone ....
the following:

TITLE	MEDIUM	SIZE	SELLING PRICE	PERCENT COMMISSION
1. ....
2. ....
3. ....
4. ....
5. ....
6. ....
7. ....
8. ....
9. ....

etc. ...... use additional sheets if necessary ....
for (purpose: e.g., sale, exhibition, inspection, etc.) to be held
from _____ (date) to _____ (date)

Until the works listed above are returned to the possession of
the Artist, each will be fully insured against loss or damage for
the benefit of the Artist in an amount not less than the selling
price less commission. None may be consigned, sent out on approval or removed during the period of the exhibition except
as agreed in writing. All of the above works are to be returned
to the Artist on demand. Reproduction rights reserved by
artist.

....
Signature of dealer-agent of gallery

....
Date

Consent is hereby given to send work out on approval:

....
Date   Signature of Artist

202

ARTISTS EQUITY—STANDARD BILL OF SALE

PLACE   DATE

(Fill out in duplicate)

Sold to: (Name) ....
   (Address) ....
      ....

Description of work: Price:

Terms of payment:

Reproduction rights reserved

(Signed) ....
    Purchaser   Artist or Authorized Dealer

APPENDIX V

AGREEMENT BETWEEN ARTIST
AND ART RENTAL OUTLET

AGREEMENT between THE ART RENTAL AND SALES GALLERY OF THE WOMAN'S BOARD OF THE ART INSTITUTE OF CHICAGO, hereinafter called "ART RENTAL", and _____, hereinafter called the "ARTIST":

1. The ARTIST may from time to time submit articles consisting of works of art to ART RENTAL for rental and sale. Any articles submitted shall have attached thereto a label prepared by the ARTIST, on a form furnished by ART RENTAL, showing the name of the ARTIST, the name of the article, if any, the media used, and the selling price of the article set by the ARTIST. It is understood that ART RENTAL has the right to reject any article submitted without giving any reason for its decision.

2. The ARTIST hereby authorizes ART RENTAL to lease any article submitted by the ARTIST and accepted by ART RENAL to any person, firm, corporation, or institution, herein referred to as the "LESSEE", for display purposes under the terms and conditions of the standard form of lease used by ART RENTAL at the time of such lease. The amount of rent to be charged shall be as follows:

Selling Price of Article	Term of the Lease	Amount of Rent
$ 50. to $ 99.	1 Rental Period	$10.00
$100. to $199.	" " "	$15.00
$200. to $299.	" " "	$20.00
$300. to $399.	" " "	$25.00
$400. to $499.	" " "	$30.00
$500. to $599.	" " "	$35.00
$600. to $699.	" " "	$40.00
$700. to $799.	" " "	$45.00
$800. to $899.	" " "	$50.00
$900. to $1,500.	" " "	$55.00

It is understood that under the terms of said lease the LESSEE has the option to renew the lease for a second term at the established rental rate.

3. Art Rental shall deduct charges of insurance and handling for each rental period and remit the balance to the ARTIST.

4. The ARTIST hereby authorizes ART RENTAL to sell any article submitted to and accepted by ART RENTAL at the selling price specified by the ARTIST on the label attached to the article as provided in paragraph 1 hereof. It is understood that under the terms of the lease used by ART RENTAL the LESSEE is given the option to purchase the article during the term of the lease, or the additional term, and to apply the rental paid against the purchase price.

5. If an article subject to the terms of this contract is sold, ART RENTAL shall remit to the ARTIST his usual 75% of the sale less rental paid to ARTIST.

6. The ARTIST shall deliver all articles at his or her expense to the place designated in Instruction Sheet.

7. ART RENTAL agrees, and each LESSEE of each article agrees in the standard form of lease now in use, not to photograph, sketch or otherwise reproduce the article and not to clean or repair the article without written permission from the ARTIST.

8. The ARTIST may withdraw any of his sketches from ART RENTAL at any time by giving five days' written notice of such withdrawal to ART RENTAL. Upon receipt of such notice the article shall be subject to return to the ARTIST as provided in paragraph 10 hereof, unless the article has been leased or sold by ART RENTAL prior to the date of receipt of such notice. If the article has been leased as aforesaid, it shall not be subject to return to the ARTIST until it has been returned to ART RENTAL by the Lessee.

9. ART RENTAL may at any time notify the ARTIST that any article of the ARTIST is subject to return to the ARTIST by sending a written notice thereof to the ARTIST in accordance with paragraph 13.

10. The ARTIST agrees to transport at his or her expense all articles to and from ART RENTAL. ART RENTAL has no duty under the terms hereof to transport the article from ART RENTAL to the ARTIST for the purpose of delivering the

same. Any article subject to return to the ARTIST as provided in paragraphs 8 or 9 hereof shall be picked up by the ARTIST, or his duly authorized agent, from ART RENTAL *within fifteen days of the date of the notice. In the event the ARTIST does not pick up said article within said period of fifteen days,* ART RENTAL shall be released from any and all responsibility for said article and may dispose of same as it seems fit.

11. ART RENTAL shall not be liable on account of any one article submitted to it by the ARTIST under the terms hereof for more than the amount of the selling price of said article set by the ARTIST as provided in paragraph 1 hereof. ART RENTAL agrees to carry insurance against loss or damage on articles submitted by the ARTIST during the period said article is in the possession of ART RENTAL.

12. This agreement shall remain in effect and governs all the transactions between ART RENTAL and the ARTIST from the date hereof until this agreement is terminated and shall be in lieu of all previous agreements. Any previous agreement between the parties on the same subject is hereby terminated. Either party may terminate this agreement at any time by thirty (30) days' written notice sent to the other party, subject, however, to the rights of any LESSEE under a lease executed by ART RENTAL in accordance with the terms hereof prior to the date notice of termination is received.

13. Any notice required or permitted under the terms of this agreement shall be in writing, sent by regular mail address to ART RENTAL AND SALES GALLERY, c/o The Art Institute of Chicago, Michigan Avenue and Adams Streets, Chicago, Illinois 60603, or to the ARTIST at the address shown on this agreement. The ARTIST may change this address when necessary by written notice to ART RENTAL giving a new address.

14. The ARTIST has examined the standard form of lease currently used by ART RENTAL.

Executed at Chicago, Illinois, ——————————— ——, 19——

———————————————————————
Artist

Address ——————————————————
Street

206

City and State   Zip Code

Tel. No. ————————————

For Art Rental and Sales Gallery of the
Woman's Board of the Art Institute of
Chicago

*(Reprinted with the permission of the Art Rental and Sales
Gallery of the Woman's Board of the Art Institute of Chicago.)*

APPENDIX VI

AGREEMENT FOR SALE OF PAINTING WITH RESERVATION OF COPYRIGHT

AGREEMENT made this .... day of ...., 19..., between .... of the City of ...., ..., party of the first part, and ...., ... of the city of ...., ..., party of the second part.

WHEREAS, the party of the first part has agreed to sell to the party of the second part a certain painting of which he is the author, and the party of the second part has agreed to purchase the same;

NOW, THEREFORE, in consideration of the mutual promises made herein and other good and valuable consideration, it is mutually agreed:

1. The party of the first part agrees to sell the painting to the party of the second part for the sum of .... ($............) Dollars, which sum the party of the second part agrees to pay to the party of the first part on delivery thereof.

2. It is further agreed that the exclusive right of reproducing such painting shall remain in the party of the first part notwithstanding its sale to the party of the second part and the copyright in the painting is hereby expressly reserved to the party of the first part, his heirs, executors, administrators and assigns.

3. The party of the second part further agrees to allow party of the first part, his heirs, executors, administrators or assigns, reasonable access to the painting which is the subject of this agreement.

IN WITNESS WHEREOF, the parties hereto have caused this agreement to be duly executed the day and year first written above.

....
....

APPENDIX VII

CODE OF ETHICS
OF THE ARTISTS EQUITY ASSOCIATION

In order to establish and build professional and public respect and confidence and to secure to the artist and the society in which he lives the benefits of economic and cultural growth, we establish this code of rights and obligations:

1. To insure high standards of conduct in the practice of the arts, and to contribute fully to the development of our American cultural heritage the creative artist must constantly strive to act so that his aims and integrity are beyond question.

2. Freedom of expression is essential for the practice of the fine arts and is the only climate in which health and growth of creative activity and discovery is possible. The artist should not, in the practice of his profession, be affected by enmities, political or religious strife, or sectarian aesthetic dissension. He should boycott professional activity involving discrimination as to race, creed or ideology.

3. The artist shall endeavor to extend public knowledge of, and respect for his profession through dedication to his work and discouragement of all untrue, unfair and distorted ideas of the role of the artist and the practice of his profession.

4. The artist shall refrain from knowingly injuring or maliciously damaging the professional reputation of work of a fellow artist.

5. He shall assume full responsibility for work completed under his direction, but freely give credit to his technical advisers and assistants.

6. When acting as juror the artist shall constantly maintain the objectivity and seriousness required for this important service, taking into account local practices and instructions from those in charge, and giving each entry as careful consideration as he would expect for his own efforts.

7. When employed as teacher, the artist shall not make exaggerated claims as to his qualifications, nor permit the school or institution in question to do so in his name.

8. The artist shall vigorously oppose vandalism, censorship

or destruction of any commissioned work of art, as well as its unauthorized commercial exploitation or defacement.

9. To avoid misunderstanding in dealings with his dealer, agent, or employer, the artist should have a written contract (with the advice of an attorney).

10. The professional artist shall utilize the protection of existing copyright laws. He should claim all fees to which he is entitled for publication and reproduction rights.

11. The artist shall fully assume his responsibility toward his client and shall not misrepresent either the value or performance of his work.

12. Before participating in charity fund-raising sales or auctions, the artist shall assure himself that works will be properly displayed, that established prices will be maintained and that he will receive whatever compensation is agreed upon.

13. The artist shall not enter competitions unless the terms are clearly stated, nor when the fees are contrary to, or below standards currently established. Except in the case of open competition he shall demand compensation for all sketches and models submitted.

14. When executing commercial, theatrical or other design commissions the artist shall familiarize himself with the codes and fair practices of allied trades to avoid misunderstandings in the execution of and remuneration for his work.

15. It is unethical for the artist to undertake a commission for which he knows another artist has been employed until he has notified such other artist and has determined that the original employment has been terminated.

APPENDIX VIII

CODE
OF FAIR PRACTICE
OF THE
JOINT ETHICS COMMITTEE

This code, sponsored by the Society of Illustrators, Inc., the Art Directors Club, Inc., The Artists Guild Inc. of New York, ASMP—The Society of Photographers in Communications, Inc., and the Society of Photographer and Artist Representatives, Inc., was first formulated in 1948 and revised in 1968.

The word artist should be understood to include creative people in the field of visual communications such as photography, graphics, film, and television.

1. Dealings between an artist or his agent and a client should be conducted only through an authorized buyer.

2. Orders to an artist or agent should be in writing and should include the price, delivery date, and a summarized description of the work. In the case of publications, the acceptance of a manuscript by the artist constitutes an order.

3. All changes or additions not due to the fault of the artist or agent should be billed to the purchaser as an additional and separate charge.

4. There should be no charges other than authorized expenses for revisions or retakes made necessary by errors on the part of the artist or his agent.

5. Alterations should not be made without consulting the artist. Where alterations or retakes are necessary and time permits and where the artist has maintained his usual standard of quality, he should be given the opportunity of making such changes.

6. The artist should notify the buyer of an anticipated delay in delivery. Should the artist fail to keep his contract through unreasonable delay in delivery, or nonconformance with agreed specifications, it should be considered a breach of contract by the artist and should release the buyer from responsibility.

7. Work stopped by a buyer after it has been started should

211

be delivered immediately and billed on the basis of the time and effort expended and expenses incurred.

8. An artist should not be asked to work on speculation. However, work originating with the artist may be marketed on its merit. Such work remains the property of the artist unless purchased and paid for.

9. Art contests except for educational or philanthropic purposes are not approved because of their speculative character.

10. There should be no secret rebates, discounts, gifts, or bonuses requested by or given to buyers by the artist or his agent.

11. If the purchase price of artwork is based specifically upon limited use and later this material is used more extensively than originally planned, the artist is to receive adequate additional remuneration.

12. If comprehensives, preliminary work or additional photographs from an assignment are subsequently published as finished art the price should be increased to the satisfaction of artist and buyer.

13. If preliminary drawings, comprehensives, or photographs are bought from an artist with the intention or possibility that another artist will be assigned to do the finished work, this should be made clear at the time of placing the order.

14. The right of an artist to place his signature upon artwork is subject to agreement between artist and buyer.

15. There should be no plagiarism of any creative artwork.

16. If an artist is specifically requested to produce any artwork during unreasonable working hours, fair additional remuneration should be allowed.

17. An artist entering into an agreement with an agent or studio for exclusive representation should not accept an order from, not permit his work to be shown by any other agent or studio. Any agreement which is not intended to be exclusive should set forth in writing the exact restrictions agreed upon between the two parties.

18. All artwork or photography submitted as samples to a buyer by artists' agents or studio representatives should bear the name of the artist or artists responsible for the creation.

19. No agent, studio, or production company should continue

212

to show the work of an artist as samples after the termination of the association.

20. After termination of an association between artist and agent, the agent should be entitled to a commission on accounts which he has secured, for a period of time not exceeding six months (unless otherwise specified by contract).

21. Examples of an artist's work furnished to an agent or submitted to a prospective purchaser shall remain the property of the artist, should not be duplicated without his consent, and should be returned to him promptly in good condition.

22. Interpretation of this code shall be in the hands of the Joint Ethics Committee and is subject to changes and additions at the discretion of the parent organizations.

APPENDIX IX

FORM G

CLASS	REGISTRATION NO.
G	DO NOT WRITE HERE
	GF GFO GP GU

Application for Registration of a Claim to Copyright in a work of art or a model or design for a work of art

Instructions: Make sure that all applicable spaces have been completed before you submit the form. The application must be SIGNED at line 11. For published works the application should not be submitted until after the date of publication given in line 6(a), and should state the facts which existed on that date. For further information, see page 4.

Pages 1 and 2 should be typewritten or printed with pen and ink. Pages 3 and 4 should contain exactly the same information as pages 1 and 2, but may be carbon copies.

Mail all pages of the application to the Register of Copyrights, Library of Congress, Washington, D.C., 20540, together with:

(a) If unpublished, a photograph or other identifying reproduction of the work and the registration fee of $6.

(b) If published, two copies of the best edition of the work (or if appropriate, photographs—see line 4) and the registration fee of $6.

Make your remittance payable to the Register of Copyrights.

1. Copyright Claimant(s) and Address(es): Give the name(s) and address(es) of the copyright owner(s). For published works the name(s) should ordinarily be the same as in the notice of copyright on the copies deposited. If initials are used in the notice, the name should be the same as appears elsewhere on the copies.

Name ....

Address ....

Name ....

Address ....

2. Title: ....

(Give the title of the work as it appears on the copies; a descriptive title may be used where the work is entirely pictorial or sculptural)

3. Nature of Work: ....

(Characterize the general type of artistic work involved, as, for example, painting, drawing, sculpture, design, model, etc.)

▶▶ NOTE: | Leave line 4 blank unless the work has been PUBLISHED and photographs deposited in lieu of copies. ◀

4. Optional Deposit: (See information on page 4.)

Basis for claiming option (Check and fill in ONE of the following):

☐ Monetary value (retail value per copy) ------

☐ Size (give dimensions) ------

☐ Weight (in pounds) ------

☐ Fragility (give details) ------

5. Author (i.e., Artist): Citizenship and domicile information must be given. Where a work is made for hire, the employer is the author. The citizenship of organizations formed under

U.S. Federal or State law should be stated as U.S.A. If the copyright claim is based on new matter (see line 7) give information about the author of new matter.

Name ------ (Give legal name followed by pseudonym if latter appears on the copies) Citizenship ------ (Name of country)

Domiciled in U.S.A. Yes ------ No ------ Address ------

➡ NOTE: Leave all spaces of line 6 blank unless your work has been PUBLISHED. ◀

6. (a) Date of Publication: Give the complete date when copies of this particular work were first placed on sale, sold, or publicly distributed. The date when copies were made or

printed should not be confused with the date of publication. (NOTE: The full date (month, day, and year) must be given.)

------ ------ ------
(Month) (Day) (Year)

(b) Place of Publication: Give the name of the country in which this particular work was first published.

(c) Manufacture Outside United States by Lithographic or Photoengraving Process: If the copies of this work were manufactured outside the United States by lithographic or photoengraving process, give the name of the country of manufacture.

➡ NOTE: Leave all spaces of line 7 blank unless the instructions below apply to your work. ◀

7. Previous Registration or Publication: If a claim to copyright in any substantial part of this work was previously registered in the U.S. Copyright Office in unpublished form, or

if a substantial part of the work was previously published anywhere, give requested information.

Was work previously registered? Yes ------ No ------ Date of registration ------ Registration number ------

Was work previously published? Yes ------ No ------ Date of publication ------ Registration number ------

Is there any substantial NEW MATTER in this version? Yes ------ No ------ If your answer is "Yes," give a brief general statement of the nature of the NEW MATTER in this version. (New matter may consist of compilation, abridgment, editorial revision, and the like, as well as additional artistic or graphic material.)

EXAMINER ☐

Complete all applicable spaces on next page

215

8. If registration fee is to be charged to a deposit account established in the Copyright Office, give name of account:

....

9. Name and address of person or organization to whom correspondence or refund, if any, should be sent:

Name .... Address ....

10. Send certificate to:

(Type or
Print
name and
address)

Name _____

Address _____

_____

_____

(City)   (State)   (ZIP code)

---

11. Certification:

(Application not
acceptable
unless signed)

I CERTIFY that the statements made by me in this application are correct to the best of my knowledge.

👉 _____

(Signature of copyright claimant or duly authorized agent)

Application Forms

Copies of the following forms will be supplied by the Copyright Office without charge upon request.

Class A Form A—Published book manufactured in the United States of America.

Class A or B { Form A–B Foreign—Book or periodical manufactured outside the United States of America (except works subject to the ad interim provisions of the copyright law).
Form A–B Ad Interim—Book or periodical in the English language manufactured and first published outside the United States of America.

Class B { Form B—Periodical manufactured in the United States of America.
Form BB—Contribution to a periodical manufactured in the United States of America.

Class D Form D—Dramatic or dramatico-musical composition.

Class E
{ Form E—Musical composition the author of which is a citizen or domiciliary of the United States of America or which was first published in the United States of America.

Form E Foreign—Musical composition the author of which is not a citizen or domiciliary of the United States of America and which was not first published in the United States of America. }

Class F Form F—Map.

Class G Form G—Work of art or a model or design for a work of art.

Class H Form H—Reproduction of a work of art.

Class I Form I—Drawing or plastic work of a scientific or technical character.

Class J Form J—Photograph.

Class K
{ Form K—Print or pictorial illustration.
Form KK—Print or label used for an article of merchandise. }

Class L
or M
{ Form L–M—Motion picture. }

Form R—Renewal copyright.

Form U—Notice of use of copyrighted music on mechanical instruments.

U.S. GOVERNMENT PRINTING OFFICE : 1968—O–310–062

FOR COPYRIGHT OFFICE USE ONLY		
Application received	Two copies received	Photographs or reproductions received
One copy or reproduction received		
Fee received		
Renewal		

Page 2

217

FORM G

CLASS	REGISTRATION NO.
G	DO NOT WRITE HERE

Certificate

Registration of a Claim to Copyright
in a work of art or a model or design for a work of art

This Is To Certify that the statements set forth on this certificate have been made a part of the records of the Copyright Office. In witness whereof the seal of the Copyright Office is hereto affixed.

Register of Copyrights
United States of America

NOT VALID WITHOUT
COPYRIGHT OFFICE
IMPRESSION SEAL

1. Copyright Claimant(s) and Address(es):

Name ....

Address ....

Name ....

Address ....

2. Title: ....

(Title of the work)

3. Nature of Work: .... (Characterize the general type of artistic work involved, as, for example, painting, drawing, sculpture, design, model, etc.)

4. Optional Deposit:

☐ Monetary value (retail value per copy) ----------------------------- ☐ Weight (in pounds) -----------------------------

☐ Size (give dimensions) ----------------------------- ☐ Fragility (give details) -----------------------------

5. Author (i.e., Artist):

Name ----------------------------- Citizenship ----------------------------- (Name of country)

(Legal name followed by pseudonym if latter appears on the copies)

Domiciled in U.S.A. Yes ------ No ------ Address -----------------------------

6. (a) Date of Publication:

----------------------------- ----------------------------- -----------------------------
(Month) (Day) (Year)

(b) Place of Publication: (c) Manufacture Outside United States by Lithographic or Photoengraving Process:

----------------------------- -----------------------------
(Name of country) (Name of country)

7. Previous Registration or Publication:

Was work previously registered? Yes ------ No ------ Date of registration ----------------------------- Registration number -----------------------------

Was work previously published? Yes ------ No ------ Date of publication ----------------------------- Registration number -----------------------------

Is there any substantial NEW MATTER in this version? Yes ------ No ------ If your answer is "Yes," give a brief general statement of the nature of the NEW MATTER in this version:

Complete all applicable spaces on next page

EXAMINER

8. Deposit account:

....

9. Send correspondence to:

Name .... Address ....

10. Send certificate to:

(Type or print name and address)

Name _____

Address _____

(Number and street)

_____

(City)   (State)   (ZIP code)

Information concerning copyright in works of art

When To Use Form G. Form G is appropriate for unpublished and published works of art, and models and designs for works of art.

What Is a "Work of Art"? This category (Class G) includes works of the fine arts, and works of artistic craftsmanship insofar as their form but not their mechanical or utilitarian aspects are concerned. Common examples of works of art are paintings, drawings, sculpture, ceramics, artistic jewelry, original designs applied to textiles, and the like.

Duration of Copyright. Statutory copyright begins on the date the work was first published, or, if the work was registered for copyright in unpublished form, copyright begins on the date of registration. In either case, copyright lasts for 28 years, and may be renewed for a second 28-year term.

Unpublished works of art

How To Register a Claim. To obtain copyright registration, mail to the Register of Copyrights, Library of Congress, Washington, D.C., 20540, a photograph or other identifying reproduction of the work, an application on Form G, properly completed and signed, and a fee of $6. Deposits are not returned, so do not send your only copy.

Published works of art

Procedure To Follow if Work Is Later Published. If the work is later reproduced in copies and published, it is necessary to make a second registration, following the procedure outlined below. To maintain copyright protection, all copies of the published edition must contain a copyright notice in the required form and position.

What Is "Publication"? Publication, generally, means the sale, placing on sale, or public distribution of copies. Unrestricted public exhibition of a work of art may also constitute publication.

How To Secure Copyright in a Published Work of Art:
1. *Produce copies with copyright notice.*
2. *Publish the work.*
3. *Register the copyright claim,* following the instructions on page 1 of this form.

The Copyright Notice. In order to secure and maintain copyright protection in a published work, it is essential that all copies published in the United States contain the statutory copyright notice. The notice should ordinarily consist of the word "Copyright," the abbreviation "Copr.," or the symbol ©, accompanied by the name of the copyright owner. The year date of publication may be included in the notice, but normally it is not required.

—*Alternative Form of Notice.* As an alternative, the notice for works of art may consist of the symbol ©, accompanied by the initials, monogram, or mark of the copyright owner, provided the owner's name appears on some accessible part of the copies.

—*Universal Copyright Convention Notice.* Use of the symbol © with the name of the copyright owner and the year date of publication may result in securing copyright in countries which are parties to the Universal Copyright Convention, which protection might not be obtained by use of either of the alternative forms of notice. Example: © John Doe 1968.

Optional Deposit. For certain published works, it may be impractical to deposit actual copies because of their size, weight, fragility, or monetary value. In such cases the Register of Copyrights may permit the deposit of photographs or other reproductions instead of the actual copies, under conditions specified in the Copyright Office Regulations. If the optional form of deposit is used, it will be necessary: (1) to fill out line 4, on pages 1 and 3, and (2) to deposit photographs or other identifying reproductions of the work. For more detailed information, write to the Copyright Office.

If you consider that first publication of your work took place by means of its unrestricted public exhibition with copyright notice, you may deposit photographs of the work.

NOTE: If copies are published without the required notice, the right to secure copyright is lost and cannot be restored.

FOR COPYRIGHT OFFICE USE ONLY		
Application received	Two copies received	Photographs or reproductions received
One copy or reproduction received		
Fee received		

U.S. GOVERNMENT PRINTING OFFICE : 1968—O-310-062

(Sept. 1968—50,000)

Page 4

Page 1

222

Application for Registration of a Claim to Copyright in a reproduction of a work of art

FORM H

CLASS	REGISTRATION NO.
H	DO NOT WRITE HERE
	HFO H

Instructions: Make sure that all applicable spaces have been completed before you submit the form. The application must be SIGNED at line 11. The application should not be submitted until after the date of publication given in line 6 (a), and should state the facts which existed on that date. For further information, see page 4.

Pages 1 and 2 should be typewritten or printed with pen and ink. Pages 3 and 4 should contain exactly the same information as pages 1 and 2, but may be carbon copies.

Mail all pages of the application to the Register of Copyrights, Library of Congress, Washington, D.C. 20540, together with 2 copies of the best edition of the work (or if appropriate, photographs—see line 4) and the registration fee of $6. Make your remittance payable to the Register of Copyrights.

1. Copyright Claimant(s) and Address(es): Give the name(s) and address(es) of the copyright owner(s). Ordinarily the name should be the same as in the notice of copyright on the copies. If initials are used in the notice, the name should be the same as appears elsewhere on the copies.

Name _____

Address _____

Name _____

Address _____

2. Title: _____
(Give the title of the work as it appears on the copies; each copy deposited should bear an identifying title)

3. Nature of Work: _____
(Characterize the general type of artistic work involved as, for example, painting, drawing, sculpture, design, model, etc.)

4. Optional Deposit: (Space 4 should be filled in *only* if the work is published and photographs are deposited in lieu of copies.
See instructions on page 4):

☐ Monetary value (retail value per copy) ----------------------- ☐ Weight (in pounds) ------------------

☐ Size (give dimensions) --

☐ Fragility (give details) --

5. Authors: Citizenship and domicile information must be given. Where a work is made for hire, the employer is the author. The citizenship of organizations formed under U.S. Federal or State law should be stated as U.S.A. If the copyright claim is based on new matter (see line 7) give information about the author of new matter.

(a) Author of the Reproduction:

Name --- Citizenship ----------------------

(Name of country)

Domiciled in U.S.A. Yes ------ No ------ Address ---

(b) Author of Original Work Which Has Been Reproduced:

Name --

6. Publication and Manufacture:

(a) Date of Publication of This Reproduction: Give the date when copies of this reproduction were first placed on sale, sold, or publicly distributed. NOTE: The full date (month, day, and year) must be given.

(b) Place of Publication of This Reproduction: Give the name of the country in which this reproduction was first published.

(c) Manufacture Outside United States by Lithographic or Photoengraving Process: If the copies of this reproduction were manufactured outside the United States by lithographic or photoengraving process, give the name of the country of manufacture.

7. New Matter In This Version: (NOTE: Leave this line blank unless the instructions apply to your work.)
If any substantial part of this work has been previously published, give a brief general statement of the nature of the new matter in this version. New matter may consist of compila- tion, revision, and the like, as well as additional graphic or artistic work.

Complete all applicable spaces on next page

EXAMINER

223

8. If registration fee is to be charged to a deposit account established in the Copyright Office, give name of account:

_____

9. Name and address of person or organization to whom correspondence and refund, if any, should be sent:

Name _____ Address _____

10. Send certificate to:

(Type or
print   Name _____
name and
address)   Address _____

_____
(Number and street)

_____
(City)   (State)   (ZIP code)

11. Certification:

(Application
not acceptable
unless signed)

> I CERTIFY that the statements made by me in this application are correct to the best of my knowledge.
>
> ☞
>
> _____
> (Signature of copyright claimant or duly authorized agent)

Application Forms

Copies of the following forms will be supplied by the Copyright Office without charge upon request.

Class A Form A—Published book manufactured in the United States of America.

{ Form A–B Foreign—Book or periodical manufactured outside the United States of America (except works subject to the ad interim provisions of the copyright law).

Class A or B { Form A–B Ad Interim—Book or periodical in the English language manufactured and first published outside the United States of America.

Class B { Form B—Periodical manufactured in the United States of America.

Form BB—Contribution to a periodical manufactured in the United States of America.

Class E { Form E—Musical composition the author of which is a citizen or domiciliary of the United States of America or which was first published in the United States of America.

Form E Foreign—Musical composition the author of which is not a citizen or domiciliary of the United States of America and which was not first published in the United States of America.

Class F   Form F—Map.

Class G   Form G—Work of art or a model or design for a work of art.

Class H   Form H—Reproduction of a work of art.

Class I   Form I—Drawing or plastic work of a scientific or technical character.

Class J   Form J—Photograph.

Class K { Form K—Print or pictorial illustration.

Form KK—Print or label used for an article or merchandise.

Class L or M } Form L-M—Motion Picture.

Form R—Renewal copyright.

Form U—Notice of use of musical composition on mechanical instruments.

FOR COPYRIGHT OFFICE USE ONLY	
Application received	
Two copies received	
Photographs or reproductions received	
Fee received	
Renewal	

☆ U.S. GOVERNMENT PRINTING OFFICE:1970—O-398-111

Page 2

225

Certificate

Registration of a Claim to Copyright
in a reproduction of a work of art

This Is To Certify that the statements set forth on this certificate have been made a part of the records of the Copyright Office. In witness whereof the seal of the Copyright Office is hereto affixed.

Register of Copyrights
United States of America

FORM H

CLASS	REGISTRATION NO.
H	DO NOT WRITE HERE

NOT VALID WITHOUT
COPYRIGHT OFFICE
IMPRESSION SEAL

1. Copyright Claimant(s) and Address(es):

Name --

Address ---

Name --

Address ---

2. Title: --

(Title of the work)

3. Nature of Work: ---------------------------------------

----

4. Optional Deposit:
Basis for claiming option:

☐ Size (give dimensions) _____

☐ Fragility (give details) _____

5. Authors:

(a) Author of the Reproduction:

Name _____ Citizenship _____
(Name of country)

Domiciled in U.S.A. Yes ____ No ____ Address _____

(b) Author of Original Work Which Has Been Reproduced:

Name _____

6. Publication and Manufacture:

(a) Date of Publication of This Reproduction: _____

(b) Place of Publication of This Reproduction: _____

(c) Manufacture Outside United States by Lithographic or Photoengraving Process: _____

_____
(Name of country)

7. New Matter In This Version: _____

_____

Complete all applicable spaces on next page

227

EXAMINER

8. Deposit account:

_____

9. Send correspondence to:

Name _____ Address _____

10. Send certificate to:

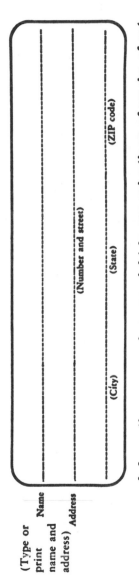

(Type or
print   Name _____
name and
address) Address _____

_____
(Number and street)

_____   _____
(City)   (State)   (ZIP code)

Information concerning copyright in reproductions of works of art

When to Use Form H. Form H is appropriate for published reproductions of works of art.

What Is a "Reproduction of a Work of Art"? This category (Class H) generally covers reproductions of existing works of art in the same or a different medium. Examples include reproductions of paintings, sculpture, or other works of art in the form of lithographs, photoengravings, etchings, drawings, etc.

Unpublished Works. A work cannot be registered as a "reproduction of a work of art" in unpublished form. Unpublished works are protected at common law against unauthorized use prior to publication.

Duration of Copyright. Statutory copyright in published reproductions lasts for 28 years from the date of first publication, and may be renewed for a second 28-year term.

How to secure statutory copyright in a reproduction of a work of art

First: Produce Copies of the Reproduction With Copyright Notice. Produce the reproduction in copies by printing or other process. To secure copyright, it is essential that the copies bear a copyright notice in the required form and position, as explained below.

Second: Publish the Reproduction With Copyright Notice. The copyright law defines the "date of publication" as ".. the earliest date when copies ... were placed on sale, or

date of publication may be included in the notice, but normally it is not required unless the work could also be regarded as a "book."

—*Alternative Form of Notice.* As an alternative, the notice for reproductions may consist of the symbol ©, accompanied by the initials, monogram, or mark of the copyright owner, provided the owner's name appears on some accessible part of the copies.

lication, mail to the Register of Copyrights, Library of Congress, Washington, D.C. 20540, two complete copies of the reproduction as published with notice, an application on Form H, properly completed and signed, and a fee of $6. NOTE: Photographs may be deposited instead of actual copies under certain circumstances; see optional deposit instructions.

The Copyright Notice. The copyright notice for reproductions should appear on the face of the work, or, if the work is a portfolio or collection of reproductions in book form, on the title page or verso thereof. It should ordinarily consist of the word "Copyright," the abbreviation "Copr.," or the symbol ©, accompanied by the name of the copyright owner. The year symbol © with the name of the copyright owner and the year date of publication may result in securing copyright in countries which are parties to the Universal Copyright Convention. Example: © John Doe 1970.

Optional Deposit. For certain published works, it may be impractical to deposit actual copies because of their size, weight, fragility, or monetary value. In such cases the Register of Copyrights may permit the deposit of photographs or other reproductions instead of the actual copies, under conditions specified in the Copyright Office Regulations. If the optional form of deposit is used, it will be necessary: (1) to fill out line 4 on pages 1 and 3, and (2) to deposit photographs or other identifying reproductions of the work.

NOTE: It is the act of publication with notice that actually secures copyright in a reproduction of a work of art. If copies are published without the required notice, the right to secure copyright is lost, and cannot be restored.

FOR COPYRIGHT OFFICE USE ONLY

Application received

Two copies received

Photographs or reproductions received

Fee received

Sept. 1970—25,000

U.S. GOVERNMENT PRINTING OFFICE:1970—O-398-111

Page 1

Application
for Registration of a Claim to Copyright
in a photograph

FORM J

REGISTRATION NO.
DO NOT WRITE HERE JPO JF JP JU

CLASS

J

Instructions: Make sure that all applicable spaces have been completed before you submit the form. The application must be **SIGNED** at line 9. For published works the application should not be submitted until after the date of publication given in line 4 (a), and should state the facts which existed on that date. For further information, see page 4.

Pages 1 and 2 should be typewritten or printed with pen and ink. Pages 3 and 4 should contain exactly the same information as pages 1 and 2, but may be carbon copies.

Mail all pages of the application to the Register of Copyrights, Library of Congress, Washington, D.C. 20559, together with:

(a) If unpublished, one complete copy of the work and the registration fee of $6.

(b) If published, two copies of the best edition of the work and the registration fee of $6.

Make your remittance payable to the Register of Copyrights.

1. Copyright Claimant(s) and Address(es): Give the name(s) and address(es) of the copyright owner(s). For published works the name(s) should ordinarily be the same as in the notice of copyright on the copies deposited. If initials are used in the notice, the name should be the same as appears elsewhere on the copies.

Name ---

Address ---

Name ---

Address ---

2. Title of Photograph: ---
(Give the title as it appears on the copies; each copy deposited should bear an identifying title, which may be descriptive)

3. Author: Citizenship and domicile information must be given. Where a work was made for hire, the employer is the ... The citizenship of organizations formed under U.S. Federal or State law should be stated as U.S.A.

If the copyright claim is based on new matter (see line 5) give information about the author of the new matter.

Name _____ Citizenship _____

_____ (Name of country)

Domiciled in U.S.A. Yes ____ No ____ Address _____

➤➤ NOTE: Leave all spaces of line 4 blank unless your work has been PUBLISHED. ◀

4. (a) Date of Publication: Give the complete date when copies of this particular photograph were first placed on sale, sold, or publicly distributed. The date when the photograph was made or the date when copies were reproduced should not be confused with the date of publication. NOTE: The full date (month, day, and year) must be given.

_____ _____ _____
(Month) (Day) (Year)

(b) Place of Publication: Give the name of the country in which this particular photograph was first published.

_____

➤➤ NOTE: Leave all spaces of line 5 blank unless the instructions below apply to your work. ◀

5. Previous Registration or Publication: If a claim to copyright in any substantial part of this work was previously registered in the U.S. Copyright Office in unpublished form, or if a substantial part of the work was previously published anywhere, give requested information.

Was work previously registered? Yes ____ No ____ Date of registration _____ Registration number _____

Was work previously published? Yes ____ No ____ Date of publication _____ Registration number _____

Is there any substantial NEW MATTER in this version? Yes ____ No ____ If your answer is "Yes," give a brief general statement of the nature of the NEW MATTER in this version. (New matter may consist of compilation, abridgment, editorial revision, and the like, as well as additional pictorial material.)

_____

Complete all applicable spaces on next page

EXAMINER

231

6. If registration fee is to be charged to a deposit account established in the Copyright Office, give name of account:

_____

7. Name and address of person or organization to whom correspondence or refund, if any, should be sent:

Name _____ Address _____

8. Send certificate to:

(Type or
print
name and
address)

Name _____

Address _____

_____
(Number and street)

_____
(City)   (State)   (ZIP code)

9. Certification:

(Application
not acceptable
unless signed)

> I CERTIFY that the statements made by me in this application are correct to the best of my knowledge.
>
> ☞ _____
> (Signature of copyright claimant or duly authorized agent)

Application Forms

Copies of the following forms will be supplied by the Copyright Office without charge upon request:

Class A   Form A—Published book manufactured in the United States of America.

Form A–B Foreign—Book or periodical manufactured outside the United States of America (except works subject to the ad interim provisions of the copyright law).

Class A or B   Form A–B Ad Interim—Book or periodical in the English language manufactured and first published outside the United States of America.

Class B   Form B—Periodical manufactured in the United States of America.

Form BB—Contribution to a periodical manufactured in the United States of America.

232

Class C — Lecture or similar production prepared for oral delivery.
Class D — Dramatic or dramatico-musical composition.

Class E
{ Form E—Musical composition the author of which is a citizen or domiciliary of the United States of America or which was first published in the United States of America.
Form E Foreign—Musical composition the author of which is not a citizen or domiciliary of the United States of America and which was not first published in the United States of America. }

Class F — Form F—Map.
Class G — Form G—Work of art or a model or design for a work of art.
Class H — Form H—Reproduction of a work of art.
Class I — Form I—Drawing or plastic work of a scientific or technical character.
Class J — Form J—Photograph.

Class K
{ Form K—Print or pictorial illustration.
Form KK—Print or label used for an article of merchandise. }

Class L or M
{ Form L–M—Motion picture. }

Class N — Form N—Sound recording.
• Form R—Renewal copyright.
• Form U—Notice of use of copyrighted music on mechanical instruments.

FOR COPYRIGHT OFFICE USE ONLY
Application received
One copy received
Two copies received
Fee received
Renewal

Page 2

233

FORM J

REGISTRATION NO.

CLASS

J

DO NOT WRITE HERE

Certificate

Registration of a Claim to Copyright

in a photograph

This Is To Certify that the statements set forth on this certificate have been made a part of the records of the Copyright Office. In witness whereof the seal of the Copyright Office is hereto affixed.

Register of Copyrights
United States of America

NOT VALID WITHOUT
COPYRIGHT OFFICE
IMPRESSION SEAL

1. Copyright Claimant(s) and Address(es):

Name

Address

Name

Address

2. Title of Photograph:

(Title of photograph as it appears on the copies)

3. Author:

(Name of country)

Domiciled in U.S.A. Yes ____ No ____ Address _____

4. (a) Date of Publication:

_____
(Month)   (Day)   (Year)

(b) Place of Publication:

_____
(Name of country)

5. Previous Registration or Publication:

Was work previously registered? Yes ____ No ____ Date of registration _____ Registration number _____

Was work previously published? Yes ____ No ____ Date of publication _____ Registration number _____

Is there any substantial NEW MATTER in this version? Yes ____ No ____ If your answer is "Yes," give a brief general statement of the nature of the NEW MATTER in this version.

_____

_____

Complete all applicable spaces on next page

EXAMINER

235

6. Deposit account:

7. Send correspondence to:

Name _____ Address _____

8. Send certificate to:

(Type or
print
name and
address)

Name _____

Address _____

_____
(Number and street)

_____
(City)   (State)   (ZIP code)

Information concerning copyright in photographs

When to Use Form J. Form J is appropriate for unpublished and published photographs.

What Is a "Photograph"? This category (Class J) includes photographic prints and filmstrips, slide films, and individual slides.

—*Reproductions.* Reproductions of photographs prepared by photolithography and other mechanical processes are generally regarded as "prints" rather than "photographs" and, when published, should be submitted for registration on Form K.

—*Contributions to Periodicals.* When a photograph is first published with a separate copyright notice in a magazine or newspaper, it is regarded as a "contribution to a periodical," registrable on Form BB.

Duration of Copyright. Statutory copyright begins on the date the work was first published, or, if the work was registered for copyright in unpublished form, copyright begins on the date of registration. In either case, copyright lasts for 28 years, and may be renewed for a second 28-year term.

Unpublished photographs

How to Register a Claim. To obtain copyright registration, mail to the Register of Copyrights, Library of Congress, Washington, D.C. 20559, one complete copy of the photograph, an application on Form J, properly completed and signed, and a fee of $6. Deposits are not required, so do not send your

Procedure to Follow if Work Is Later Published. If the photograph is later reproduced in copies and published, it is necessary to make a second registration, following the procedure outlined below. To maintain copyright protection, all copies of the published edition must contain a copyright notice in the

Published Photographs

What Is "Publication"? Publication, generally, means the sale, placing on sale, or public distribution of copies. Unrestricted public exhibition of a photograph may also constitute publication.

How to Secure Copyright in a Published Photograph:
1. *Produce copies with copyright notice.*
2. *Publish the work.*
3. *Register the copyright claim,* following the instructions on page 1 of this form.

The Copyright Notice. In order to secure copyright protection in a published work, it is important that all copies contain the statutory copyright notice. The notice should appear on the photograph itself, or, if the work is a collection of photographs in book form, on the title page or verso thereof. It should ordinarily consist of the word "Copyright," the abbreviation "Copr.," or the symbol ©, accompanied by the name of the copyright owner. The year date of publication may be included in the notice, but normally it is not required unless the work could also be regarded as a "book."

—*Alternative Form of Notice.* As an alternative, the notice for photographs may consist of the symbol ©, accompanied by the initials, monogram, or mark of the copyright owner, provided the owner's name appears on some accessible part of the copies.

—*Universal Copyright Convention Notice.* Use of the symbol © with the name of the copyright owner and the year date of publication may result in securing copyright in countries which are parties to the Universal Copyright Convention. Example: © John Doe 1973.

NOTE: If copies are published without the required notice, the right to secure copyright is lost and cannot be restored.

FOR COPYRIGHT OFFICE USE ONLY		
Application received		
One copy received		
Two copies received		
Fee received		

U.S. GOVERNMENT PRINTING OFFICE: 1973-O-507-231   Aug. 1973—40,000

237

FORM K

REGISTRATION NO.	CLASS
DO NOT WRITE HERE KF KFO K	**K**

Application
for Registration of a Claim to Copyright
in a print or pictorial illustration

Instructions: Make sure that all applicable spaces have been completed before you submit the form. The application must be SIGNED at line 10. The application should not be submitted until after the date of publication given in line 5(a), and should state the facts which existed on that date. For further information, see page 4.

Pages 1 and 2 should be typewritten or printed with pen and

ink. Pages 3 and 4 should contain exactly the same information as pages 1 and 2, but may be carbon copies.

Mail all pages of the application to the Register of Copyrights, Library of Congress, Washington, D.C. 20559, together with 2 copies of the best edition of the work (or if appropriate, photographs—see line 3) and the registration fee of $6. Make your remittance payable to the Register of Copyrights.

1. Copyright Claimant(s) and Address(es): Give the name(s) and address(es) of the copyright owner(s). Ordinarily the name(s) should be the same as in the notice of copyright on the copies deposited. If initials are used in the notice, the name should be the same as appears elsewhere on the copies.

Name ....

Address ....

Name ....

Address ....

2. Title: ....

(Give the title of the work as it appears on the copies; a descriptive title may be used where the work is entirely pictorial)

➤ **NOTE:** | Leave line 3 blank unless photographs are deposited in lieu of copies. | ◀

3. Optional Deposit: (See instructions on page 4.)
Basis for claiming option (Check and fill in **ONE** of the following):

☐ Monetary value (retail value per copy) .... ☐ Weight (in pounds) ....

☐ Size (give dimensions) .... ☐ Fragility (give details) ....

the information must be given. Where a work is made for as U.S.A. If the copyright claim is based on new matter (see hire, the employer is the author. The citizenship of organiza- line 6), give information about the author of new matter.

Name .... Citizenship .... (Name of country)

(Give legal name followed by pseudonym if latter appears on the copies)

Domiciled in U.S.A. Yes ...... No ...... Address ....

5. (a) Date of Publication of the Print or Illustration: Give the date when copies of this print or illustration were first placed on sale, sold, or publicly distributed. The date when

copies were made or printed should not be confused with the date of publication. NOTE: The full date (month, day, and year) must be given.

....
(Month)   (Day)   (Year)

(b) Place of Publication: Give the name of the country in which this print or illustration was first published.

....

(c) Manufacture Outside United States by Lithographic or Photoengraving Process: If the copies of this reproduction were manufactured outside the United States by lithographic or photoengraving process, give the name of the country of manufacture.

....

➤➤ **NOTE:** | **Leave all spaces of line 6 blank unless the instructions below apply to your work.** ◄◄

6. Previous Registration or Publication: If a claim to copy- right in any substantial part of this work was previously reg- istered in the U.S. Copyright Office in unpublished form, or

if a substantial part of the work was previously published anywhere, give requested information.

Was work previously registered? Yes ...... No ...... Date of registration .... Registration number ....

Was work previously published? Yes ...... No ...... Date of publication .... Registration number ....

Is there any substantial NEW MATTER in this version? Yes ...... No ...... If your answer is "Yes," give a brief general statement of the nature of the NEW MATTER in this version. (New matter may consist of compilation, revision, and the like, as well as additional pictorial or graphic work.)

....

EXAMINER

Complete all applicable spaces on next page

239

7. If registration fee is to be charged to a deposit account established in the Copyright Office, give name of account:

....

8. Name and address of person or organization to whom correspondence and refund, if any, should be sent:

Name .... Address ....

9. Send certificate to:

(Type or print name and address)

Name ....

Address ....

....
(Number and street)

....
(City)   (State)   (ZIP code)

10. Certification:

(Application not acceptable unless signed)

I CERTIFY that the statements made by me in this application are correct to the best of my knowledge.

☞ ....
(Signature of copyright claimant or duly authorized agent)

Application Forms

Copies of the following forms will be supplied by the Copyright Office without charge upon request. :

Class A   Form A—Published book manufactured in the United States of America.

Class A   Form A–B Foreign—Book or periodical manufactured outside the United States of America (except works subject to
or B   the ad interim provisions of the copyright law).
           Form A–B Ad Interim—Book or periodical in the English language manufactured and first published outside the
           United States of America.

Class B   Form B—Periodical manufactured in the United States of America.
          Form BB—Contribution to a periodical manufactured in the United States of America.

240

Form E—Musical composition the author of which is a citizen or domiciliary of the United States of America or which was first published in the United States of America.

Class E
Form E Foreign—Musical composition the author of which is not a citizen or domiciliary of the United States of America and which was not first published in the United States of America.

Class F   Form F—Map.
Class G   Form G—Work of art or a model or design for a work of art.
Class H   Form H—Reproduction of a work of art.
Class I   Form I—Drawing or plastic work of a scientific or technical character.
Class J   Form J—Photograph.
Class K   Form K—Print or pictorial illustration.
          Form KK—Print or label used for an article of merchandise.
Class L
or M   Form L-M—Motion picture.
Class N   Form N—Sound recording.
   • Form R—Renewal copyright.
   • Form U—Notice of use of copyrighted music on mechanical instruments.

FOR COPYRIGHT OFFICE USE ONLY	
Application received	
Two copies received	
Photographs or reproductions received	
Fee received	
Renewal	

U.S. GOVERNMENT PRINTING OFFICE : 1973—O—499-473

FORM K

REGISTRATION NO.

DO NOT WRITE HERE
KF   KFO   K

CLASS

K

Certificate
Registration of a Claim to Copyright
in a print or pictorial illustration

This Is To Certify that the statements set forth on this certificate have been made a part of the records of the Copyright Office. In witness whereof the seal of the Copyright Office is hereto affixed.

Register of Copyrights
United States of America

NOT VALID WITHOUT
COPYRIGHT OFFICE
IMPRESSION SEAL

1. Copyright Claimant(s) and Address(es):

Name ....

Address ....

Name ....

Address ....

2. Title: ....

(Title of the work)

3. Optional Deposit:
Basis for claiming option:

☐ Monetary value (retail value per copy) .... ☐ Weight (in pounds) ....

☐ Size (give dimensions) .... ☐ Fragility (give details) ....

4. Author of the Print or Illustration:

Name ------------ (Legal name followed by pseudonym if latter appears on the copies) ------------ Citizenship ------------ (Name of country)

Domiciled in U.S.A. Yes ----- No ----- Address ------------

5. (a) Date of Publication of the Print or Illustration:

------------ (Month) ------------ (Day) ------------ (Year)

(b) Place of Publication:

------------ (Name of country)

(c) Manufacture Outside United States by Lithographic or Photoengraving Process:

------------ (Name of country)

6. Previous Registration or Publication:

Was work previously registered? Yes ----- No ----- Date of registration ------------ Registration number ------------

Was work previously published? Yes ----- No ----- Date of publication ------------ Registration number ------------

Is there any substantial **NEW MATTER** in this version? Yes ----- No ----- If your answer is "Yes," give a brief general statement of the nature of the **NEW MATTER** in this version.

Complete all applicable spaces on next page

EXAMINER

243

7. Deposit account:

8. Send correspondence to:

Name ....   Address ....

9. Send certificate to:

(Type or
print   Name ....
name and
address) Address ....

(Number and street)

(City)   (State)   (ZIP code)

Information concerning copyright in prints and pictorial illustrations

When to Use Form K. Form K is appropriate for published prints and pictorial illustrations.

What Is a "Print or Pictorial Illustration"? This category (Class K) includes prints and pictorial illustrations produced by lithography, photoengraving, or other methods of reproduction. Examples: greeting cards, picture postcards, calendar illustrations, and the like.

Unpublished Works. A work cannot be registered as a "print or pictorial illustration" in unpublished form. Unpublished works are protected at common law against unauthorized use prior to publication.

Duration of Copyright. Statutory copyright in published prints and pictorial illustrations lasts for 28 years from the date of first publication, and may be renewed for a second 28-year term.

How to secure statutory copyright in a print or pictorial illustration

First: Produce Copies With Copyright Notice. Produce the print or illustration in copies by printing or other means of reproduction. To secure copyright, it is essential that the copies bear a copyright notice in the required form and position, as explained below.

Second: Publish the Work With Copyright Notice. The copyright law defines the "date of publication" as ". . . the

but normally it is not required unless the work could also be regarded as a "book."

—*Alternative Form of Notice.* As an alternative, the notice for prints and illustrations may consist of the symbol ©, accompanied by the initials, monogram, or mark of the copyright owner, provided the owner's name appears on some accessible part of the copies.

earliest date when copies . . . were placed on sale, sold, or publicly distributed."

Third: Register Your Copyright Claim. Promptly after publication, mail to the Register of Copyrights, Library of Congress, Washington, D.C. 20559, two complete copies of the print or illustration as published with notice, an application on Form K, properly completed and signed, and a fee of $6. NOTE: Photographs may be deposited instead of actual copies under certain circumstances; see optional deposit instructions.

The Copyright Notice. The copyright notice for prints and pictorial illustrations should appear on the face of the work, or, if the work is a portfolio or collection of prints in book form, on the title page or verso thereof. It should ordinarily consist of the word "Copyright," the abbreviation "Copr.," or the symbol ©, accompanied by the name of the copyright owner. The year date of publication may be included in the notice,

—*Universal Copyright Convention Notice.* Use of the symbol © with the name of the copyright owner and the year date of publication may result in securing copyright in countries which are parties to the Universal Copyright Convention. Example: © John Doe 1973.

Optional Deposit. For certain published works, it may be impractical to deposit actual copies because of their size, weight, fragility, or monetary value. In such cases the Register of Copyrights may permit the deposit of photographs or other reproductions instead of the actual copies, under conditions specified in the Regulations of the Copyright Office. If the optional form of deposit is used, it will be necessary: (1) to fill out line 3 on pages 1 and 3, and (2) to deposit photographs or other identifying reproductions of the work. For more detailed information, write to the Copyright Office.

NOTE: It is the act of publication with notice that actually secures copyright protection in a print or pictorial illustration. If copies are published without the required notice, the right to secure copyright is lost, and cannot be restored.

FOR COPYRIGHT OFFICE USE ONLY	
Application received	
Two copies received	
Photographs or reproductions received	
Fee received	

U.S. GOVERNMENT PRINTING OFFICE: 1973—O-499-473   June 1973—50,000

245

APPENDIX XIII

ASSIGNMENT OF COPYRIGHT

I, JOHN DOE, represent that I am the owner and author of all rights in an original artistic work entitled, —————, which has been copyrighted solely by me.

In consideration of the sum of $—————, I hereby assign to REPRODUCTIONS LIMITED, INC., all of my right, title and interest in and to said work and in the copyright thereon, together with the right to secure renewals, reissues and extensions of such copyright.

I also sell, assign and transfer all of the claims and demands which I might have against all persons who may have heretofore infringed any of the rights, previous claims and demands under said copyright.

This assignment shall extend to the full term remaining of the copyright, any renewal or extension thereof.

Dated this ————— day of —————, 19—————.

—————————————————————
John Doe

Accepted and Approved
REPRODUCTIONS LIMITED, INC.

By: —————————————————————

246

APPENDIX XIV

RELEASE

In consideration of $_____ and other good and valuable consideration paid to me by _____ ("artist" "photographer"), receipt of which is acknowledged, I hereby consent for all purposes to the sale, reproduction and/or use of a portrait, picture or photograph of (with or without the use of my name), by the ("artist" "photographer") and by any of their nominees or designees in all forms and media and in all manners, including advertising, trade, display, editorial, art and exhibition.

In giving this consent, I hereby release the ("artist" "photographer") his nominees and designees from liability for any violation of any personal or proprietary right I may have in connection with such sale, reproduction or use.

I am of legal age.

(signed) _____

Witness: _____

Date: _____

GUARDIAN'S CONSENT (if applicable)

I am the parent and guardian of the minor named above and have the legal authority to execute the above consent and release. I approve the foregoing and waive any rights in the premises.

(signed)_____

Witness: _____

Date: _____

APPENDIX XV

APPLICATION FOR EXPERT OPINION
AS TO AUTHENTICITY

Whitney Museum of American Art   Date _____
945 Madison Avenue
New York, N.Y.

Gentlemen:

This is to confirm that I own the work of art which I have described below, that I have requested an opinion concerning such work from a member of the staff of the Whitney Museum of American Art, that I have not requested such opinion in connection with any past or contemplated commercial transaction, that I understand that in agreeing that such an opinion may be given the Museum is relying on the foregoing statements, that no fee has been requested for such opinion and that I have not paid any such fee.

In consideration of your agreement to have a member of the Museum's staff examine such work and render an opinion, which may be oral or written, as to, among other things, its authorship, I hereby (a) agree that neither such opinion nor its communication to any other person will be made the grounds for any suit, in law or equity, on any theory whatsoever against the Museum, against any of its Trustees or any member of its staff or against any third person consulted in connection with such opinion, (b) release each and every claim which I may now or hereafter have which might serve as the basis for any such suit and (c) indemnify and agree to hold harmless the Museum, its Trustees and every member of its staff and every such third person for any damages or expenses it, he or she may suffer as the result of any such suit brought by any other party on the grounds of such opinion or its communication to any other person.

If such work is delivered to the Museum for such examination, I further agree to pay all transportation charges to and

248

from the Museum and to collect such work promptly upon the Museum's request. I also agree that such work, from the date it leaves my possession until received back by me, shall be delivered to and from the Museum and left with it entirely at my risk, and that the Museum shall not be responsible for any loss or damage to such work while in its possession or in transit, and that the Museum shall not cover it with insurance.

I further agree to furnish the Museum with a clear black and white photograph of the work, to be kept by the Museum.

Yours truly,

_____

Address _____

Telephone Number _____

Artist_____ Title _____

Medium _____Dimensions _____

Previous history (from whom acquired, with address, and date acquired; and any known information as to history and any exhibitions and publications in which it may have been included). If necessary, use reverse side.

(Reprinted with permission of the Whitney Museum of American Art)

APPENDIX XVI

CONDITIONS OF SALE AT AUCTION

CONDITIONS OF SALE

This printed catalogue, as amended by any posted notices or oral announcements during the sale, constitutes Sotheby Parke Bernet, Inc.'s (the "Galleries") and the "Consignor's" entire statement relative to the property listed herein. The following Conditions of Sale, any glossary contained herein and the accompanying Terms of Guarantee set forth herein are the complete terms and conditions on which all property listed herein shall be offered for sale, sold or purchased. The property will be offered and sold by the Galleries normally as agent for the Consignor.

1. The authenticity of the Authorship of property listed in the catalogue is guaranteed as specifically stated in the Terms of Guarantee. Except as so specifically provided in the "Terms of Guarantee" with respect to authenticity of Authorship, all property is sold "as is" and neither the Galleries nor the Consignor makes any warranties or representations of any kind or nature with respect to, nor shall they be held responsible or liable for the correctness of the catalogue or other description of the physical condition, size, quality, rarity, importance, provenance, exhibitions, literature and historical relevance of the property and no statement in the catalogue or made at the sale or in the bill of sale or invoice or elsewhere shall be deemed such a warranty or representation or an assumption of liability with respect thereto. Prospective bidders should inspect the property before bidding to determine its condition and whether or not it has been repaired or restored. The Galleries and the Consignor make no representation or warranty expressed or implied as to whether the purchaser acquires any reproduction rights in the property.

2. The Galleries reserves the right to withdraw any property at any time before actual sale.

3. Unless otherwise announced by the auctioneer at the time of sale all bids are per lot as numbered in the printed catalogue.

4. The Galleries reserves the right to reject a bid from any

bidder. The highest bidder acknowledged by the auctioneer shall be the purchaser in the event of any dispute between bidders, the auctioneer shall have sole and final discretion either to determine the successful bidder or to re-offer and resell the article in dispute. If any dispute arises after the sale, the Galleries' sale record shall be conclusive in all respects.

5. If the auctioneer determines that any opening bid is not commensurate with the value of the article offered, he may reject the same and withdraw the article from sale, and if, having acknowledged an opening bid, he decides that any advance thereafter is not of sufficient amount he may reject the advance.

6. On the fall of the auctioneer's hammer, the highest bidder shall be deemed to have purchased the offered lot in accordance with all of the conditions set forth herein and thereupon (a) assumes full risk and responsibility therefor, (b) will sign a confirmation of purchase thereof, and (c) will thereupon pay the full purchase price therefor or such part as the Galleries may require. All property shall be removed from the Galleries by the purchaser at his expense not later than three (3) days following its sale and, if not so removed, may be sent by the Galleries to a public warehouse for the account, risk and expense of the purchaser. If the foregoing Conditions or any other applicable conditions herein are not complied with, in addition to other remedies available to the Galleries and the Consignor by law, including without limitation the right to hold the purchaser liable for the bid price, the Galleries, at its option may either (a) cancel the sale, retaining as liquidated damages all payments made by the purchaser or (b) resell the property on three (3) days notice to the purchaser and for the account and risk of the purchaser, either publicly or privàtely, and in such event the purchaser shall be liable for the payment of deficiency plus all of the costs, including warehousing, the expenses of both sales, and the Galleries' commission on both sales at its regular rates and all other charges due hereunder and incidental damages.

7. Unless the sale is advertised and announced as a sale without reserves, each lot is offered subject to a reserve and the Galleries may implement such reserves by bidding through its representatives on behalf of the Consignor. In certain instances,

251

the Consignor may pay the Galleries less than the standard commission rate where a lot is "brought-in" to protect its reserve. Where the Consignor is indebted to or has a monetary guarantee from the Galleries, and in certain other instances, the Galleries or affiliated companies may have an interest in the offered lots and the proceeds therefrom other than their commissions, and may bid therefor to protect such interests by a representative or agent.

8. Unless exempted by law from the payment thereof, the purchaser will be required to pay the combined New York State and local sales tax. The rate of such combined tax is 7 percent if within New York City and ranges from 4 percent to 7 percent if outside New York City but within New York State.

Deliveries outside of New York State may be subject to the compensating use tax of another state and, where a duty of Collection is imposed upon them by law, the Galleries will require payment of such taxes.

GLOSSARY

The following are examples of the terminology used in this catalogue. PLEASE NOTE THAT ALL STATEMENTS IN THIS CATALOGUE AS TO AUTHORSHIP, PERIOD, CULTURE, SOURCE OR ORIGIN ARE QUALIFIED STATEMENTS AND ARE MADE SUBJECT TO THE PROVISIONS OF THE CONDITIONS OF SALE AND THE "TERMS OF GUARANTEE."

a "JACQUES-LOUIS DAVID"—followed, under the heading "AUTHORSHIP," by the words "ascribed to the named artist." The work is ascribed to the named artist either by an outside expert or by our own staff and such ascription is accepted as reliable by the Galleries. While this is our highest category of authenticity in the present catalogue, and is assigned only upon exercise of our best judgment, no unqualified statement as to authorship is made or intended.

b ATTRIBUTED TO JACQUES-LOUIS DAVID
In our best judgment, the work can be ascribed to the artist on the basis of style, but less certainty as to authorship is expressed than in the preceding category.

c CIRCLE OF JACQUES-LOUIS DAVID

In our best judgment, a work by an unknown hand closely associated with the named artist.

d STUDIO OF JACQUES-LOUIS DAVID
In our best judgment, a work by an unknown hand executed in the style of the artist under his direct supervision.

e SCHOOL OF . . . ; FOLLOWER OF JACQUES-LOUIS DAVID
In our best judgment a work by a pupil or follower of the artist.

f MANNER OF JACQUES-LOUIS DAVID
In our best judgment a work in the style of the artist, but not by him and probably of a later period.

g AFTER JACQUES-LOUIS DAVID
In our best judgment a copy of a known work of the artist.

h SIGNED
A work which has a signature which in our best judgment is a recognized signature of the artist.

i DATED
A work which is so dated and in our best judgment was executed at that date.

TERMS OF GUARANTEE

The Galleries guarantees the authenticity of Authorship of each lot contained in this catalogue on the terms and conditions set forth below:

1. *Definition of Authorship*

"Authorship" means the identity of the creator, the period, culture, source or origin of the property, as the case may be, as set forth in the BOLD TYPE HEADING of each catalogue entry.

2. *Guarantee Coverage*

Subject to the exclusions of (i) attributions of paintings, drawings or sculpture executed prior to 1870, and (ii) periods or dates of execution of the property, as explained in Paragraph 5 below, if within five (5) years from the date of the sale of any lot, the original purchaser of record tenders to the Galleries a purchased lot in the same condition as when sold through the Galleries and it is established that the identification of Authorship (as defined above) of such lot as set forth in the BOLD TYPE HEADING of the catalogue description of such lot (as

253

amended by any posted notices or oral announcements during the sale) is not substantially correct based on a fair reading of the catalogue including the terms of any Glossary contained herein, the sale of such lot will be rescinded and the original purchase price refunded.

3. *Non-Assignability*

It is specifically understood that the benefits of this Guarantee are not assignable and shall be applicable only to the original purchaser of the lot from the Galleries and not to the subsequent owners or others who have or may acquire an interest therein.

4. *Sole Remedy*

It is further specifically understood that the remedy set forth herein, namely the rescission of the sale and refund of the original purchase price paid for the lot, is exclusive and in lieu of any other remedy which might otherwise be available as a matter of law.

5. *Exclusions*

The Guarantee covers only the correctness of description of Authorship (as defined in 1 above) as identified in the BOLD TYPE HEADING of the catalogue item but does *not* extend to (i) the identity of the creator of paintings, drawings and sculpture executed before 1870 unless these works are determined to be counterfeits, as this is a matter of current scholarly opinion which can change, (ii) the identification of the periods or dates of execution of the property which may be proven inaccurate by means of scientific processes not generally accepted for use until after publication of the catalogue, or (iii) titles or other identification of offered lots or descriptions of physical condition and size, quality, rarity, importance, provenance, exhibitions and literature of historical relevance, which information normally appears in lower-case type below the BOLD TYPE HEADING identifying the Authorship. Although our best judgment is used in attributing paintings, drawings and sculpture created prior to 1870 through the appropriate use of glossary terms, and due care is taken to insure the correctness of the supplemental material which appears below the BOLD TYPE HEADING of each entry in the catalogue, the Guarantee does not extend to any possible errors or omissions therein.

(Reprinted with Permission of Sotheby Parke Bernet, Inc.)

APPENDIX XVII

RENTAL AGREEMENT

Due ――――――――
Due ――――――――

Standard term ends 2 months from date.

Dated   19

LEASE

THE ART RENTAL AND SALES GALLERY OF THE WOMAN'S BOARD OF THE ART INSTITUTE OF CHICAGO, Lessor, hereby leases

to ―――――――――――――― Lessee, for

a ―――――― term, at a rental of $――――――

the following described article:

Artist's name: ――――――――――――

Title of Work: ――――――――――――

Medium ―――――― Condition ――――――

for display at the Lessee's address shown herein, and for no other use or purpose whatsoever.

Lessee acknowledges receipt of the article in good condition

255

unless otherwise indicated on this lease, and agrees to return it in the same condition at the expiration of this lease. Lessee shall not clean or repair the article or remove it from its frame or base or in any other way alter it. Acceptance by Lessor of the return of the article shall not be construed as a waiver of any claim it may have for damage to the article prior to the return thereof even though works are insured by Lessor.

Lessee or Purchaser agrees not to sketch, photograph, reproduce or otherwise use the article for advertising or commercial purposes, or permit any other person to do so without written permission of the artist. Lessee shall not sublease the article or assign this lease.

Lessee may: (a) extend this lease subject to the same conditions, for one additional term by paying to Lessor the established rental rate prior to the expiration of the original term of this lease: (b) purchase the article, during the terms of this lease or during the additional term, if the lease is extended as provided herein, by paying to Lessor, as agent of the artist, $ _____ less the amount of rental paid, (excluding additional insurance premium, if any) plus sales tax.

Lessor may terminate this lease at any time by giving fifteen days' written notice by registered or certified mail to Lessee, at the address shown herein. In the event of termination, Lessor shall refund to Lessee, on return of the article as provided herein, a pro-rata portion of the prepaid rental allocable to the unexpired portion of the rental term.

Upon termination of this lease by lapse of time or otherwise, Lessee agrees to return the article, at Lessee's expense and suitably wrapped or crated for transit, to Lessor at the Receiving Dock, Monroe Street entrance of the Art Institute of Chicago, between 9:00 A.M. and 5:00 P.M., Mondays through Saturdays, except legal holidays. If Lessee fails to return the article when due, Lessee shall pay to Lessor as liquidated damages a sum equal to twice the amount of the rental thereof, pro-rated per day for the whole time possession of the article is withheld, plus any cost or expense incurred by Lessor in recovering possession thereof, and Lessor or its agents are expressly authorized to enter the premises of Lessee and to remove the article without penalty or liability for trespass at any time after expiration of this lease.

ART RENTAL AND SALES GALLERY OF THE WOMAN'S BOARD, THE ART INSTITUTE OF CHICAGO

_____
Lessee's signature

_____
Address

_____
City and State   Zip Code

BY: _____

_____
Residence Phone

_____
Business Phone

(Reprinted with the permission of the Art Rental and Sales Gallery of the Woman's Board of the Art Institute of Chicago.)

CUSTOMER ART CONTRACT

KULICKE FRAMES, INC.
43 EAST 10th STREET, NEW YORK, NEW YORK 10003
43 EAST 78th STREET, NEW YORK, NEW YORK 10021
TELEPHONE (212) AL 4-0140

**THIS DOCUMENT IS A CONTRACT BETWEEN THE CUSTOMER AND KULICKE FRAMES, INC.
SUBJECT TO THE TERMS AND CONDITIONS SET FORTH ON BACK OF FORM.
READ IT CAREFULLY.**

REC'D
FROM:

name

street

city

tel. no.

BILL
TO:

name

street

city

tel. no.

DATE	RECEIVED BY	LOCATION RECEIVED	ATTENTION	RETURN TO CUSTOMER	ORDER #
		10th 78th			

RECEIVED UNOPENED

PACKAGE (S) VIA

CONDITION

QTY.	CODE #	ARTIST	TITLE	MEDIUM/ DESCRIPTION	CONDITION	SIZE	ADD. VALUE OVER $50 INSURANCE PURCHASED

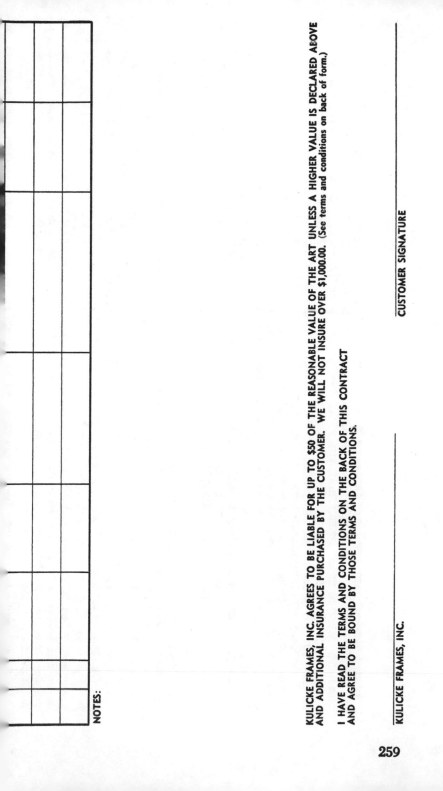

NOTES:

KULICKE FRAMES, INC. AGREES TO BE LIABLE FOR UP TO $50 OF THE REASONABLE VALUE OF THE ART UNLESS A HIGHER VALUE IS DECLARED ABOVE AND ADDITIONAL INSURANCE PURCHASED BY THE CUSTOMER. WE WILL NOT INSURE OVER $1,000.00. (See terms and conditions on back of form.)

I HAVE READ THE TERMS AND CONDITIONS ON THE BACK OF THIS CONTRACT AND AGREE TO BE BOUND BY THOSE TERMS AND CONDITIONS.

KULICKE FRAMES, INC. _____

CUSTOMER SIGNATURE _____

259

1. LIMITATION OF LIABILITY AND INSURANCE KULICKE FRAMES, INC. IS NOT LIABLE FOR ANY ART LEFT WITH US UNLESS A FRAME ORDER IS CONFIRMED OR PRIOR ARRANGEMENTS ARE MADE IN WRITING. IN CONSIDERATION OF THE RATE CHARGED IT IS AGREED THAT THE VALUE OF THE ART LEFT WITH US IS NOT MORE THAN $50.00, AND THE LIABILITY OF KULICKE FRAMES, INC. FOR LOSS OR DAMAGE, IRRESPECTIVE OF THE CAUSE OF SUCH LOSS OR DAMAGE, INCLUDING NEGLIGENCE, IS LIMITED TO $50.00 UNLESS A GREATER VALUE IS DECLARED AND AN INCREASED CHARGE FOR INSURANCE BASED UPON SUCH GREATER VALUE IS PAID. THE CHARGE FOR ADDITIONAL INSURANCE IS $1.00 FOR EVERY $100.00 OR ANY FRACTION THEREOF OF EXTRA VALUE. IT IS AGREED THAT NO ART WILL BE LEFT WITH KULICKE FRAMES, INC. UNLESS THE VALUE IS STATED AT THE TIME OF DELIVERY. IF, AFTER NOTICE TO KULICKE FRAMES, INC. AND THE PURCHASE OF ADDITIONAL INSURANCE, HIGH VALUE ITEMS ARE ACCEPTED BY KULICKE FRAMES, INC. THE LIABILITY OF KULICKE FRAMES, INC. SHALL BE LIMITED TO THE AMOUNT OF INSURANCE PURCHASED. IN NO EVENT SHALL ANY ART BE INSURED FOR MORE THAN ITS REASONABLE VALUE. FAILURE TO COMPLY WITH THE TERMS HEREIN SHALL RELIEVE KULICKE FRAMES, INC. OF ALL LIABILITY OVER $50.00 FOR LOSS OR DAMAGE TO ART WORK IRRESPECTIVE OF THE CAUSE OF LOSS OR DAMAGE, INCLUDING NEGLIGENCE.

2. HOLDING ART WORK/CANCELLATION OF ORDERS If an order cannot be executed for any reason, Kulicke Frames, Inc. reserves the right to return art work at the customer's expense. Art work held for frame orders for which we require and are awaiting payment will be held for only 30 days, and if no payment is received within that time, the order is considered cancelled. There is a minimum of $10.00 service charge in addition to all storage charges and delivery charges accrued thereon for handling art which is not framed or for orders which are cancelled. All art work left for a period of time exceeding 30 days without specific instructions or advance payment for framing will be subject to sale, either public or private, without notice to the owner thereof. Kulicke will not hold art work valued at $1,000.00 or more longer than 24 hours for fitting purposes.

3. ART HANDLING Kulicke Frames, Inc. recognizes and follows the highest standards of art handling and conservation. However, certain work is uninsurable and is done entirely at the customer's risk. We are not liable for damage to art requiring restoration, repair, stretching, trimming, flattening, keying out or any other special handling. Art of uncertain media, fragility, vulnerability or age will be receipted only at the customer's risk.

We cannot accept responsibility for the phenomenon of rippling, buckling or warping of art work on paper which is framed. Ad-

4. PLAS-PAR-TOUT: IMPORTANT NOTICE We do not accept responsibility for any art, reproductions, graphics, photographs, or any other item left with us for the Plas-Par-Tout process, NOR CAN ADDITIONAL INSURANCE BE PURCHASED TO COVER WORK LEFT WITH US FOR THIS PROCESS.

5. COMPLETION OF ORDERS Notification will be given when a frame order is completed. Unclaimed merchandise and art remaining with us for more than 60 days after notification of completed framing will be deemed abandoned and will be subject to sale, either public or private, without notice to the owner thereof. There will be a storage charge for all orders kept beyond 60 days. If merchandise and art cannot be sold within a period of 6 months from the date upon which it becomes subject to sale as herein provided Kulicke may dispose of said merchandise and art by making a gift thereof.

6. SHIPPING AND DELIVERY WE ASSUME NO LIABILITY FOR HANDLING OR DAMAGE DURING PICK UP OR DELIVERY. Completion and delivery dates are approximate. CLAIMS FOR DAMAGE TO ART WORK OR FRAMES MUST BE MADE TO KU-LICKE FRAMES, INC. IN WRITING WITHIN SEVEN (7) DAYS OF THE CUSTOMER'S RECEIPT OF THE MERCHANDISE AND CLAIMS NOT MADE WITHIN SEVEN (7) DAYS SHALL BE DEEMED WAIVED. Our liability for art and frames ceases when they are accepted for packing or delivery by an independent carrier or agent. We accept no returns unless authorized, and claims for loss or damage in transit must not be withheld from the payment of our invoices. Independent carriers must be notified at once in writing of all claims for damage, and all wrapping materials must be retained until such claims are settled.

7. PRICES Sizes on certain items are restricted beause of material limitations, and there is a 10% surcharge on frames over 48" in any dimension. All prices quoted are estimated and are subject to office verification. Price lists are subject to change without notice. All payment is due on completion of order.

8. PICK UP Under no circumstances will Kulicke Frames, Inc. pick up an art work unless our customer art contract is signed by the owner or his authorized representative prior to pick up or when pick up is made. The customer is responsible for properly packaging art work for pick up and transit. Packaging by our driver is done entirely at the customer's own risk. In no event do we assume any responsibility for damage to art during pick up or in transit.

(Reprinted with Permission of Kulicke Frames, Inc.)   261

WHITNEY MUSEUM OF AMERICAN ART / LOAN AGREEMENT

945 Madison Avenue, New York, N.Y. 10021 (212) 249-4100

Please complete, sign and return. The blue copy is for your records.

EXHIBITION

Lender _____ Telephone (Business) ( ) Area Code
                                              (Home) ( )

Address _____
(Unless otherwise instructed below, work will be shipped from and returned to this address)

Credit _____
(Exact form of lender's name for catalogue, labels and publicity)

Name of Artist _____ Born _____ Died _____
                                        (year)   (year)

Address of Artist _____

Title of Work _____

Medium or Materials and Support _____

Size: Painting, drawing, etc. (excl. frame or mat): H _____ W _____ Outer dimensions of frame: H _____ W _____

Sculpture (excl. pedestal) or relief: H _____ W _____ D _____ Approx. Wt. _____

Pedestal: H _____ W _____ D _____ Approx. Wt. _____ Detachable? _____

Date of Work _____ If date appears on work, where? _____

Signature If work is signed, where?

Is Work for Sale? _____ **Selling Price** _____ (See conditions on the reverse)

Insurance Value (U.S. Currency) $ _____
(See conditions on the reverse; insurance cannot exceed selling price, if any)

Do you prefer to maintain your own insurance? _____ If so, estimated premium _____

Framing: Is the work framed? _____ If necessary, may we reframe or remat the work? _____ May we substitute plexiglas for glass? _____

The work will be returned to the lender in its original frame or mat unless other arrangements are made with the Museum in writing.

Photographs: Which of the following are available: Black and white photographs for catalogue reproduction and publicity? (If known,

please give negative number) _____ Color separations or plates? _____ Transparencies? _____

Color slides, post cards or other reproductions for sale? _____

Unless permission is declined here, it is understood that this work may be photographed, telecast and reproduced for publicity purposes connected with this exhibition and for illustration in the Museum's catalogue and other publications, and that slides of it may be made and distributed for educational use.

Special Instructions: Ship from _____ Return to _____ Other _____

Duration of Loan: ☐ at Whitney Museum only; ☐ at Whitney Museum and subsequent tour.

THE CONDITIONS OF THIS LOAN AS STATED ABOVE AND ON THE REVERSE ARE ACCEPTED.

Signed: _____ Date: _____
(Lender or authorized agent)

263

CONDITIONS

1. The Whitney Museum of American Art (the "Museum") will exercise the same care with respect to the work of art referred to on the reverse (the "work") as it does in the safekeeping of comparable property of its own.

2. The work shall remain in the possession of the Museum and/or the other museums participating in the exhibition for which it has been borrowed (the "participating museums") for the time specified on the reverse, but may be withdrawn from such exhibition at any time by the Director or Trustees of the Museum and/or of any of the participating museums. The work will be returned only to the owner or lender at the address stated on the reverse unless the Museum is notified in writing to the contrary. If the legal ownership of the work shall change during the pendency of this loan, whether by reason of death, sale, insolvency, gift or otherwise, the new owner may, prior to its return, be required to establish his legal right to receive the work by proof satisfactory to the Museum.

3. The Museum will insure the work wall-to-wall under its fine-arts policy for the amount specified by the lender on the reverse against all risks of physical loss or damage from any external cause while in transit and on location during the period of this loan; provided, however, that if the work shall have been industrially fabricated and can be replaced to the artist's specifications, the amount of such insurance shall be limited to the cost of such replacement. If no amount shall have been specified by the lender, the Museum will insure the work at its own estimated valuation. The Museum's fine-arts policy contains the usual exclusions for loss or damage due to war, invasion, hostilities, rebellion, insurrection, confiscation by order of any Government or public authority, risks of contraband or illegal transportation and/or trade, nuclear damage, wear and tear, gradual deterioration, moths, vermin and inherent vice, and for damage sustained due to and resulting from any repairing, restoration or retouching process unless caused by fire and/or explosion. The lender agrees that, in the event of loss or damage, recovery shall be limited to such amount, if any, as may be paid by the insurer, hereby releasing the Museum, each of the participating museums, and the Trustees, officers, agents and employees of the Museum and of each of the participating museums from

264

insurance naming the Museum and each of the participating museums as an additional assured or waiving subrogation against the Museum and each of the participating museums. If the lender shall fail to supply the Museum with such a certificate, this loan agreement shall constitute a release of the Museum and of each of the participating museums from any liability in connection with the work. The Museum cannot accept responsibility for any error or deficiency in information furnished to the lender's insurer or for any lapses in coverage.

5. The Museum assumes the right, unless specifically denied by the lender, to examine the work by all modern photographic means available. Information thus gathered will remain confidential and will not be published without the written consent of the lender. It is understood that the Museum will not clean, restore, or otherwise alter the work without the consent of the lender.

6. The Museum's right to return the work shall accrue absolutely at the termination of the loan. If the Museum, after making all reasonable efforts and through no fault of its own, shall be unable to return the work within sixty days after such termination, then, the Museum shall have the absolute right to place the work in storage, to charge regular storage fees and the cost of insurance therefor, and to have and enforce a lien for such fees and cost. If, after five years, the work shall not have been reclaimed, then, and in consideration for its storage, insurance and safeguarding during such period, the work shall be deemed an unrestricted gift to the Museum.

7. If the work is for sale and is sold during the period of this loan, the lender shall pay the following amount to the Museum to be used exclusively for the Museum's Art Purchase Fund: 5% of the selling price on a sale to another institution; on any other sale, 10% of the first $25,000 of the selling price and 5% of the selling price, if any, in excess of $25,000.

(Printed with Permission of the Whitney Museum of American Art)

267